A STUDENT'S APPROACH TO WORLD RELIGIONS

Islam

Victor W. Watton

*(Head of Religious Studies,
Stockton Sixth Form College)*

SERIES EDITOR : BRIAN E. CLOSE

HODDER
EDUCATION
AN HACHETTE UK COMPANY

ACKNOWLEDGEMENTS

The publishers would like to thank the following for permission to reproduce material in this volume:

American Trust Publications for extracts from *The Lawful and the Prohibited in Islam*, Yusuf al-Quaradawi; Cambridge Unviersity Press for extracts from *Islamic History - A New Interpretation, Volume 1*, M.A.Shaban, 1971; Element Books Ltd for extracts from *The Elements of Sufism*, Shaykh Fadhalla Haeri, 1990; Islamic Propagation Centre International for extracts from *The Holy Koran*, Yusuf Ali (trans); Muslim Educational Trust for extracts from *Islam: Beliefs and Teachings*, Ghulam Sarwar, 1989; extracts from *Muhammad*, Michael Cook, 1983 and *Muhammad, Prophet and Statesman*, Montgomery Wall, 1960, by permission of Oxford University Press; Routledge & Kegan Paul for extracts from *Islamic Spirituality*, S. Nasr (ed.), 1987, *Muslims: their Religious Beliefs and Practices, Volume 1*, A Rippin, 1990, *The Qur'an and its Exegesis*, H Gatje, 1976 and *The World's Religions*, Sutherland, Houlden, Clarke and Hardy (eds), 1988; Ta-Ha Publishers Limited for extracts from *Dajjal The King who has no clothes*, Ahmad Thomson, 1986; The Open Press Ltd for extracts from *Hajj in Focus*, Zafarul-Islam Khan and Yaqub Zaki (eds), 1986; Volcano Press Ltd for extracts from *Islam in Britain - Past, Present and Future*, Mohammad S. Raza, 1991; Yale University Press for extracts from *An Introduction to Shi'i Islam*, Moojan Momen, 1985, © 1985 by Moojan Momen.

Every effort has been made to trace and acknowledge ownership of copyright. The publishers will be glad to make suitable arrangements with any copyright holders whom it has not been possible to contact.

To my wife and children –
Jill, Simon, Rebecca, Timothy, Abigail and Peter.

Orders: please contact Bookpoint Ltd., 130 Milton Park, Abingdon, Oxon OX14 4SB.
Telephone: (44) 01235 827720, Fax: (44) 01235 400454.
Lines are open from 9.00-5.00, Monday to Saturday, with a 24 hour message answering service.
You can also order through our website: www.hoddereducation.co.uk

British Library Cataloguing in Publication Data
Watton, Victor W.
Islam. - (Student s Approach to World Religions Series)
I. Title
II. Series
297

ISBN : 978 0 340 58795 9

First published 1993
Impression number   22
Year   2014

Typeset by Western Printing Services Ltd., Bristol
Printed and bound by CPI Group (UK) Ltd, Croydon, CR0 4YY for Hodder Education, an Hachette UK Company, 338 Euston Road, London NW1 3BH

CONTENTS

*On their first appearance, Arabic words are in italic.
Subsequently they appear in normal type.*

INTRODUCTION

Islam is the religion of over eight hundred million people around the world. The countries of the Middle East, North Africa, Central Asia and Indonesia have majority Muslim populations and several have Muslim constitutions and legal systems. Nineteenth century European colonialism led to emigration between East and West as a result of which there are now growing Muslim communities in Western Europe and North America.

The word Islam comes from the Arabic word for submission, but is also connected with *salaam* meaning peace. Islam is the religion of submission to the will of God which, Muslims believe, is the only way to bring peace between people and with God. A Muslim is one who has submitted to God's will.

Clearly, if Islam is submission to God's will and it is believed that this will bring peace to the world, it follows that Islam has to be a complete way of life. Muslims believe that God's will was revealed in its final and complete form in the word of God, the *Qur'an*, given by God to Muhammad between 610 CE and 632 CE. The Qur'an covers all aspects of life and, in combination with the example and teachings of Muhammad, forms a holy law *(Shari'a)* which Muslims must follow.

Islam is a complete way of life, and its concepts of peace and submission make it very much a community religion. In his final sermon to Muslims shortly before he died, Muhammad said, 'Every Muslim is a brother to every other Muslim', so that at the heart of Islam is belief in human equality and concern for your fellow human beings. Being a Muslim is not just a matter of your relationship with God, it is also a way of life in which a Muslim tries to make this world the sort of place God intended it to be.

As this book is intended to help A level students understand Islam, it does not only give the fundamental teachings of Islam, but also conflicting ideas of modern Muslim scholars and Western scholars (often referred to in Muslim books as orientalists). Most Muslims would disagree with such ideas as they believe there are no conflicts or divisions within Islam. The ordinary Pakistani, Bangladeshi or Arab Muslim believes that Islam as he/she practises it is pure Islam, which all Muslims all over the world believe and practise.

The spelling of words used in Islam can cause many problems. The generally accepted spellings have been used, and a few of the variations can be found in the glossary. Mecca and Medina have been used as being more familiar than the more accurate *Makkah* and *Madinah*. God has been used rather than *Allah* to emphasise to the non-Muslim reader that Muslims worship God and not some other being.

All quotations from the Qur'an are taken from *The Holy Qur'an - A Translation and Commentary*, Yusuf Ali, available from the Islamic Propogation Centre, Birmingham. This is the translation most acceptable to Muslims in the UK. Rather than using footnotes, each quotation is identified by the name of the author and the book source can be found either after the quotation or in the recommended reading list provided for each chapter.

Rather than using the Islamic dating system of AH (after the *hijra* of Muhammad to Medina in 622 CE), the Common Era (CE and BCE) has been used as this is used in most books on Islam. AH has difficulties because there is no simple method of converting AH to CE since the Muslim system of a year equalling twelve lunar months means that every 32 years AH becomes a whole solar year behind CE. This can be seen in the fact that 1993 CE is 1414 AH rather than 1371AH.

CHAPTER ONE

THE QUR'AN

It is often thought by Christians that Islam is similar to Christianity and therefore, that Muhammad occupies the same status in Islam that Jesus has in Christianity. Christians believe that Jesus came directly from God and that Jesus told the world everything they need to know about God. Jesus is God in the world. He is actually called 'the Word of God made flesh'. Muslims do not believe any of these things about Muhammad, but they do believe that the Qur'an is a direct revelation of God. The Qur'an is God's word and is the nearest thing there is to a part of God in the world.

So the Qur'an is the most important thing in Islam. God has revealed his word to people in this book which tells Muslims everything they need to know about God, religion and how to live their lives. The Qur'an occupies a similar place in Islam to that occupied by Jesus in Christianity.

> The Qur'an is the complete book of guidance for mankind. It is the sacred book of the Muslims and the main source of law in Islam. The whole of the Qur'an is from Allah. Each word of it is a revealed word. (*Islam:Beliefs and Teachings*, Ghulam Sarwar)

The Origins of the Qur'an

To understand the Qur'an you have to go right back to the beginnings of the earth.

According to Islam, God created humans to be his vice-regents on earth i.e. Adam was God's first prophet whose task was to look after the world in the way God wanted it to be looked after. Clearly to do this Adam needed instructions from God and those instructions were given as God's word. Unfortunately, subsequent generations distorted the word and so other messengers had to be given the word again.

According to Islam, there have been several written books of the word of God; *Musa* (Moses) was given the *Tawrat* (Torah - first five books of the Bible); *Dawud* (David) was given the *Zabur* (Psalms); *Isa* (Jesus) was given the *Injil* (Gospel). Unfortunately, none were given in such a way that they could not be distorted.

Muslims believe that when God saw that the Injil was totally distorted (especially in saying Jesus was God's son), he decided to send his word in such a form that it could never be distorted. To do this, he chose Muhammad because he had all the characteristics God wanted in his final messenger. Most important of all, although Muhammad was highly intelligent, he could not read or write. This meant that God could give Muhammad his word as a dictation which Muhammad could learn by heart and so could not distort it.

According to Islam, when God called Muhammad, he did not tell him to go and preach, or perform miracles, he said, 'Proclaim (or read) in the name of thy Lord and Cherisher who created man out of a clot of congealed blood ' (sura 96). The key word here is 'Proclaim' (more usually translated as recite). If you recite, you are repeating the words of someone else, you are not saying your own words. That was what Muhammad did, he recited the words God gave him, so the Qur'an (which can mean recitation in Arabic) is the word of God, not the word of Muhammad.

There are various examples in the biographies of Muhammad of how the revelations of the Qur'an came to him. Apparently he often heard the ringing of a bell and then his brow was covered in sweat as God communicated with him. There are some differences between Muslim scholars on exactly how the revelations were given, with some saying that they did not come directly from God, but had to be given by the angel *Jibrail* (Gabriel) because even Muhammad could not have direct communication with God. It seems from the Qur'an that some of the revelations were given by Jibrail, but that most came directly from God.

So the origin of the Qur'an was as the final word of God to the people of the earth given *via* Muhammad. He was God's prophet who merely recited what God told him.

There is a lack of clarity amongst Muslim authors about whether or not the holy books given before the Qur'an were **the Qur'an** which then became distorted. The classic teaching is that the Qur'an is eternal - 'an earthly copy of a heavenly original', and that to be a Muslim you need to know, believe and follow all that is in the Qur'an. This would seem to imply that each of the holy books **was** the Qur'an and, therefore, **all** the prophets were true Muslims.

However, several Muslim scholars believe that the earlier holy books were **not** the Qur'an, they only had certain parts of the Qur'an in them. Only the Qur'an, as revealed to Muhammad, contains the complete form of God's word.

> We have been commanded to believe in previously revealed Books only in the sense of admitting that, before the Qur'an, God had also sent down books through His Prophets, that they were all from the same God, the God who sent the Qur'an, and the sending of the Qur'an... confirms, restates and completes those divine instructions. (Abul Ala Mawdudi)

The Compilation of the Qur'an

The revelations of the Qur'an to Muhammad began in 610CE and continued until just before the Prophet's death i.e. 632CE.

During this time, it appears that at first the Prophet got his followers to learn the revelations by rote (memory). At a later stage he had secretaries to whom he dictated the revelations and they wrote them down on whatever came to hand (the traditions mention bits of leather and pottery as well as scraps of paper). The Prophet checked these to make sure they were exactly what God had said and then they were put into a chest which was kept by his wife Hafsa (the daughter of Umar). In 631CE, Muhammad went through the chest and sorted the revelations into suras (some of which are suras because they were all revealed at the same time, others were separate revelations put together because they were about a similar theme). Unfortunately, the Prophet died before he could sort the suras out into chronological order, so there are 114 suras, but there is no record of which came first.

The importance of learning by memory can be seen in the respect and reverence given in early Islam to the professional remembrancers who had learnt the whole Qur'an directly from the Prophet. However, because the Qur'an was believed to be the word of God and it contained all the regulations of Islam, it was important to be absolutely sure what was 'the word'. Consequently, two years after Muhammad's death the Caliph Abu Bak'r ordered the Prophet's chief secretary, Zayd ibn Thabit to make an official version of the Qur'an from the documents in Hafsa's chest. This complete written Qur'an was given into the safekeeping of Hafsa.

However, during the reign of Umar other written Qur'ans were made from the statements of the remembrancers and there were at least four versions in circulation. None of these versions had any record of chronology and so it was impossible to tell which verse had appeared first. Since certain verses of the Qur'an supersede others (e.g. there are verses which say prayer can be made facing any direction and others which say prayer must be made facing Mecca) it was important that there should be no variations and so the Caliph Uthman ordered all the Prophet's secretaries to meet together and make an official copy of the Qur'an based on Hafsa's documents. This was done in 652CE (20 years after the Prophet's death) and all other copies of the Qur'an were destroyed.

As a result of Uthman's work, all Qur'ans in existence have 114 suras, 77,639 words and 323,015 letters. There are differences between Qur'ans in the organisation of the *ayat* (verses) but no differences at all in the words.

The problem of contradictory statements in the Qur'an raised by certain verses superseding others was solved by the notion that a revelation could be made for a specific time or situation and then expanded or refined or even abolished by a subsequent revelation.

This teaching, made it important to discover the chronology of the suras. Initially, Muslim scholars did this on the distinction between Meccan and Medinan suras and by comparing the suras with events in Muhammad's life. However, as Helmut Gatje says, 'The results of traditional Muslim research are not satisfying and one must accept the fact that definitive decisions regarding exact dates or, even exact chronological order, are simply no longer possible.'

For most Muslims, this is not a problem. The *Sunna* of Muhammad and the Shari'a of Islam convey quite clearly which verses supersede and which are superseded.

Uthman organised the Qur'an in order of length with the exception of sura 1 which is a call to worship and is the part of the Qur'an which features most regularly in the prayer ritual of *Salah*. So sura 2 is the longest sura and sura 114 is the shortest. Every sura except sura 9 begins with the *Bismillah* ('In the name of God the Merciful, the Compassionate'). This indicates that the whole Qur'an comes from God. Each sura is recited in the name of God, not the name of Muhammad. Muslims believe that each sura is a sign of God's compassion and mercy because he has not left them alone to get on with their lives, but has given them the Qur'an so that they know how to live. They believe that if they follow what the Qur'an teaches, then they will go to heaven, but if they ignore it, they will end up in hell.

So the Qur'an has a very different history from the Bible. It was all revealed to one person, it was revealed over a period of 21 years and written down within another 21 years and there are no differences between texts of the Qur'an: the Bible on the other hand was revealed to many people over a period of 1500 years, did not achieve its final written form until 300 years after the final revelation and there are many differences between texts of the Bible. Muslims feel that this shows the Qur'an is the final word of God.

This is the Muslim view of the origin and compilation of the Qur'an. It has, however, been challenged recently by some Western scholars. In 1971, Helmut Gatje pointed out that the Kufic Arabic script, in which early Qur'ans were written, had no vowels and that when vowels were put in, there was a possibility of mistakes as one different vowel could give a word a totally different meaning.

Andrew Rippin suggested in 1990 that the belief in the Qur'an as the unalterable word of God developed during the first 200 years of Islam as a result of a conflict between Caliphs and theologians over who should determine the Shari'a. The Caliphs claimed it as their traditional right, but the theologians claimed only God could, and indeed had, through the Qur'an. It was the victory of the theologians, according to Rippin, which led to the authorised Arabic Qur'an with vowels being regarded as 'an earthly copy of a heavenly original.' Such attitudes are totally unacceptable to Muslims. As far as they are concerned the Arabic Qur'an as we have it today is exactly the same word of God, in exactly the same form as Muhammad received it.

The Authority of the Qur'an

The Qur'an itself says that it is a revelation from God which sums up all people need to know about God and religion, 'This is the Book, in it is guidance sure without doubt to those who fear God '(sura 2 v 2).

It was given to Muhammad in such a way that it can never be distorted, 'He sent among them an Apostle from among themselves, rehearsing unto them the Signs of God, sanctifying them and instructing them in Scripture and wisdom, while before that they had been in manifest error.'(sura 3 v 164)

All these beliefs mean that, as far as Muslims are concerned, the Qur'an has absolute authority. If the Qur'an says something, then if you are a good Muslim, you must do it. As Abul Ala Mawdudi said, 'Belief in the Qur'an should be of the nature that it is purely and

absolutely God's own words, that it is perfectly true, that every word
of it is preserved, that everything mentioned therein is right...'

Muslim Attitudes to the Qur'an

It clearly follows from the nature and authority of the Qur'an that it is
the most holy thing a Muslim can possess. Therefore, most Muslims
will keep their Qur'an wrapped up so that it does not become
polluted; they will always keep it on a shelf higher than all other
books; they will not read it without first washing their hands. Muslims
will not eat, drink or involve themselves in casual conversation while
reading the Qur'an and will never let it rest below their navel. In the
mosque (where most Muslims go to read the Qur'an) special Qur'an
stands are provided so that you can read the Qur'an whilst sitting on
the floor without the Qur'an touching the floor.

All these regulations apply to the Arabic Qur'an. Muslims believe that
Arabic is the language of God because it is the language in which the
Qur'an was revealed and as it is eternal, Arabic must be the language
of God. An English translation of the Qur'an is not **the Qur'an**, it is an
interpretation, only the Arabic version is **the Qur'an** . All Muslims
must therefore learn to read the Qur'an in Arabic and in non-Arabic
speaking countries children go to mosque school to learn to read
Arabic (they learn to read the Qur'an in Arabic even though they may
not understand it). Pious Muslims learn the Qur'an off by heart so
they can recite it all (they are then called a *hafiz*). However, Muslims in
the UK are now being encouraged to read Qur'ans with Arabic and
English side by side (as in the Yusuf Ali translation) so that they
understand what they read, and there are many text books to help
Muslim children understand their religion.

Why do Muslims Believe the Qur'an is the Word of God ?

Apart from the basic teachings on the Qur'an, Muslim scholars put forward several reasons for believing that the Qur'an is the word of God

1   It is the only miracle which Muhammad performed and all prophets perform a miracle.

2   It is written in the most beautiful Arabic possible as the Qur'an says 'And if ye are in doubt as to what We have revealed from time to time to Our servant, then produce a sura like thereunto and call your witnesses... but of a surety ye cannot,'(sura 2 v 23). There is also a story of a great Arabic poet at the time of Muhammad, Labid ibn Rabia, who had one of his poems pinned on the wall of the Ka'ba; it was so good that no one dared pin another poem next to it, but one night someone pinned a verse of the Qur'an next to it and the next day Rabia read the verse and tore his own poem down and became a Muslim because the poetry of the Qur'an was so good.

3   Muhammad was illiterate and so he could not have written the Qur'an himself.

4   There are no differences between the different copies of the Qur'an, therefore, it must be the word of God.

5   The sayings of Muhammad himself, *Hadith*, are kept separate from the Qur'an and so Muhammad and his followers must have been aware that there was a total difference between what Muhammad said and the words of the Qur'an

6   The language of the Qur'an is so beautiful that the very sound of it can convert people:

> The sacred quality of the psalmody of the Qur'an can cause spiritual rapture even in a person who knows no Arabic. In a mysterious way, this sacred quality is transmitted across the barriers of human language and is felt by those hundreds of millions of non-Arab Muslim, whether they be Persian, Turkish, African, Indian or Malay, whose hearts palpitate in the love of God and whose eyes are moistened by tears of joy upon simply hearing the Qur'an chanted. (Seyyed Hossein Nasr)

The Contents of the Qur'an

Some scholars have claimed that the Qur'an was primarily a book of prophecy. By this they mean that it contains warnings about a future judgement and indications of when that judgement will be. It is true that the short suras do tend to be concerned very much with judgement.

Nevertheless, even the short suras tend to be concerned with what a Muslim should believe and how they should live their life,' Until there should come to them clear evidence, an Apostle from God, rehearsing scriptures kept pure and holy: wherein are laws right and straight.' (sura 98 v 2,3) This is even clearer in the longer suras and from this one can assert that the Qur'an is a book of guidance about what to believe and what to do.

The Qur'an contains all the fundamental Muslim beliefs about God; 'Say He is God, the One and Only God, the Eternal, Absolute; He begetteth not nor is He begotten; And there is none like unto Him.' (sura 112); about creation, 'God is He Who raised the heavens without any pillars that ye can see... And it is He who spread out the earth and set thereon mountains standing firm and flowing rivers and fruit of every kind.' (sura 13 v 2,3); about the afterlife, 'On that day will she declare her tidings: for that thy Lord will have given her inspiration. On that Day will men proceed in companies sorted out, to be shown the deeds that they had done. Then shall anyone who has done an atom's weight of good, see it! And anyone who has done an atom's weight of evil shall see it.' (sura 99)

The Qur'an gives stories from the lives of the prophets, 'Remember Abraham and Ismail raised the foundations of the House (Ka'ba)' (sura 2 v 127); 'Has the story of Moses reached thee? Behold he saw a fire so he said to his family "Tarry ye: I perceive a fire; perhaps I can bring you some burning brand therefrom, or find some guidance at the fire." But when he came to the fire, a voice was heard, "O Moses! Verily I am thy Lord! Therefore put off thy shoes: thou art in the sacred valley." ' (sura 20 v 9-12); 'Then will God say, "O Jesus the son of Mary! Recount My favour to thee and to thy Mother. Behold! I strengthened thee with the holy spirit so that thou didst speak to the people in childhood and maturity. " ' (sura 5 v 113)

It teaches about prayer, 'O ye who believe! When ye prepare for prayer, wash your faces and your hands and arms up to the elbow; rub your heads with water and wash your feet to the ankles... and call in remembrance the favour of God.' (sura 5 v 7, 8) ; about fasting,

'Ramadan is the month in which was sent down the Qur'an, as a guide to mankind, also clear signs for guidance and judgement between right and wrong. So everyone of you who is present at his home during that month should spend it in fasting.' (sura 2 v 185); about *Zakah*, 'Alms are for the poor and the needy.' (sura 9 v 60); about *Hajj*, 'The first House of Worship... pilgrimage thereto is a duty men owe to God - those who can afford the journey.'(sura 3 v 96-7)

It explains the nature of morality, 'It is not righteousness that ye turn your faces towards East or West; but it is righteousness - to believe in God and the Last Day, and the angels and the Book, and the Messengers; to spend of your substance out of love for Him, for your kin, for orphans, for the needy, for the wayfarer, for those who ask and for the ransom of slaves; to be steadfast in prayer, and practise regular charity;' (sura 2 v 177).

So the Qur'an is a book about what Muslims should believe and how they should behave, much of which originally appeared in prophetic forms.

The Nature and Status of Hadith

Although the Qur'an is regarded as complete and unalterable, like any other book there can be different ideas about what different passages mean. There are also some items which are not covered by the Qur'an. To help them with these difficulties, Muslims refer to Muhammad. The Qur'an is the most important guide for Muslims, but obviously if you need help, the final Prophet who was given the word must be the one to turn to. What Muhammad said the Qur'an meant, or what Muhammad did or said, must be the next best guide to the Qur'an.

A good example is with Salah. The Qur'an tells you to pray at first light, midday, afternoon and evening, facing Mecca having first washed, but it does not tell you what to do or say. For this Muslims use the Sunna (example) of the Prophet and Hadith (what he said).

Sunna and Hadith are the second source of behaviour for a Muslim. If the Qur'an is not clear, then you look at the Sunna or Hadith of the Prophet and follow that.

The problem with Hadith is that there is no **one** authorised version and so there are differences and contradictions between Hadith. A Muslim scholar, Bukhari, recognised this problem and made a collection of 600,000 Hadith in the ninth century which he then subjected to scrutiny. He determined that only those Hadith with a genuine *isnad* (list of guarantors e.g. *'Munsif told me that he had heard from Ali who had heard Muhammad say'*) going back to one of the Companions of the Prophet could be accepted as correct. In this way he reduced the number of Hadith from 600,000 to 7,000.

Most Muslims accept that the *Hadith of Bukhari* are genuine because of the isnad guarantee, but there are several other collections of Hadith which some Muslims prefer to Bukhari's e.g. *Sahih Muslim, Sunan abu Dawud, Sunan ibn Majah*. Some use the same isnad method as Bukhari, some not. These four collections are the basis of the Shari'a which is looked at in detail in chapter five.

A typical Hadith goes as follows:

> On the authority of Abu Hamza Anas ibn Malik (may Allah be pleased with him), the servant of the Messenger of Allah (may the blessings and peace of Allah be upon him) that the Prophet said, 'None of you truly believes until he wishes for his brother what he wishes for himself.' It was related by al'Bukhari and Muslim (An' Nawari's *Forty Hadith*)

Despite these collections, there are some modern Muslims who distrust Hadith because they are not the word of God and they will only follow the Qur'an. They claim that the Qur'an is the word of God which cannot be distorted. The Hadith, because of their history could have been distorted.

Nevertheless, the vast majority of Muslims accept the Hadith and Sunna of the Prophet and feel that they must obey them. They believe that the Hadith have been kept pure, and that as Muhammad was the final prophet, his words and example offer Muslims the perfect way to live. They would not place Hadith on a par with the Qur'an, but they would place them one step down.

> As the Qur'an is the word of Allah, it must be strictly followed: in the same way, the teachings contained in the Prophet's Sunna must be observed by all who profess to be Muslims, for about them the Holy Qur'an says,'And whatsoever the Messenger giveth you, take it. And whatever he forbiddeth, abstain from it.' Thus the Sunna in the form of Hadith is complementary to the Holy Book itself: it helps to explain and clarify the Holy Qur'an and to present practical application of its teachings. Without a study of Hadith a Muslim's knowledge of his faith remains incomplete, (translators' introduction to *Forty Hadith*).

CHAPTER TWO

THE SIX BELIEFS OF ISLAM

The idea that Islam can be summed up in six beliefs is based on a Hadith which says, 'You must believe in Allah, his angels, his holy books, his messengers, in the Last Day and life after death.'

Many modern Muslim text books reduce these six beliefs to three:- *tawhid*, which is belief in the unity of God, but includes all the other Muslim beliefs about God; *risalah*, which literally means God's messengers, but also includes belief in angels and holy books; *akirah*, which means the Last Things and includes beliefs about the Last Day and life after death.

These are the basic beliefs of Islam, but they are by no means the only ones. **Islam means submission and therefore a Muslim must also believe in the Pillars and Shar'ia as a sign of submission to God's Will.**

There are two other beliefs which are sometimes regarded as essential beliefs of Islam. These are *Jihad* (struggling for God which some regard as a sixth pillar) and *al'Qad'r* (God's control of everything - predestination, which some regard as a seventh belief).

1. Tawhid

Muslim scholars realised from the beginning that the fact that God is called Allah (the God) in Arabic tells you a lot about the Muslim concept of God. Firstly, Allah is simply the Arabic word for God and is not the name for some other being. Secondly, Allah has no plural in Arabic. It cannot be made to refer to more than one and so the very fact that the Qur'an says Allah means that there is only one God.

The supreme importance of tawhid for modern Muslims is explained by Seyyed Hossein Nasr,

> Allah is first and before everything else One, and it is the Oneness of God that lies at the centre of both the Qur'anic doctrine of God and Islamic spirituality... Islamic mystical treatises as well as

theological ones based on the text of the Qur'an and hadith are essentially one long commentary on the divine oneness and its meaning.

As far as many Muslims are concerned, sura 112 explains the whole of God's nature, 'In the name of God, Most Gracious, Most Merciful say, "He is God the One and Only, God the Eternal, Absolute. He begetteth not nor is He begotten; and there is none like unto Him."'

This means that God has always been in existence and will always be in existence. It also means that, as far as Muslims are concerned, Christians totally misunderstand the nature of God because they claim that God begot Jesus Christ and that rather than being One, God is Three (the Christian doctrine of the Trinity). This is shown in the Qur'anic verse, 'They do blaspheme who say, "God is Christ the Son of Mary"... Whoever joins other gods with God - God will forbid him the Garden.' (sura 5 v 75)

Muslim belief in God's unity also means that the beliefs of Arabian Polytheism must have been wrong. Polytheism is totally condemned in the Qur'an, 'Have ye seen Lat and Uzza and another the third goddess Manat?... These are nothing but names which ye have devised... it is to God that the end and beginning of things belong.' (sura 53 v 19 - 25)

Implications of God's Oneness in Muslim Life

The total importance of belief in the unity of God for Muslims can be seen in the fact that the worst sin a Muslim can commit is the sin of *shirk* (associating other beings with God). Anyone who commits shirk can no longer be considered a Muslim for it is the one unforgivable sin

There are no pictures in any mosques because of tawhid. The only art you find is calligraphy or geometric patterns. In *Sunni* homes there are no pictures of the Prophet or any of his helpers and some very strict Muslims do not even allow photographs. The belief is that any form of representational art might lead you to worship the art rather than your creator.

For some Muslims the concept of shirk is so strong that they oppose Western capitalism because it leads to Muslims worshipping their material possessions rather than putting God first and this is also shirk. 'So it is with a believer. When he surrenders himself to Allah alone, he can go forward in the affairs of this life without fear. But if he does not obey Allah, he has to obey false gods like the fear of losing his job, fear of danger, fear of hunger and the like.' (Ghulam Sarwar)

The oneness of God is the first thing a Muslim baby hears when his/ her father recites the *Shahada* into their ear as soon after birth as possible. These words should also be on their lips as they die, showing that they are Muslim.

The Creativity of God

Clearly if God is one with no helpers and no associates, then Muslims must believe that the world in which we are living is his creation. In other words a concomitant belief of the oneness of God is the creativity of God: 'It is He who created for you all things that are on earth; moreover His design comprehended the heavens.' (sura 2 v 29)

God's creative power is total, 'To Him is due the primal origin of the heavens and the earth: when He decreeth a matter, He saith to it, "be" and it is' (sura 2 v 117).

In fact the Qur'an contains several verses which use the 'Design' argument to show the power and creativity of God i.e. they point to how life is organised and see these as signs of God's creativity and his love for the world. 'Behold! In the creation of the heavens and the earth, and the alternation of night and day, these are indeed signs for men of understanding.' (sura 3 v 190)

Modern Muslims have extended this Qur'anic teaching to the ideas of science and claim that because science shows the universe working according to laws there is a unity about the universe: stars and planets, life itself have a common origin, a common purpose because the universe was created by one 'Absolute' power - Allah.

Such a view tends to ignore the teaching of the Qur'an of how God created the earth and put Adam and Eve in the Garden of Eden, 'Verily your Lord is God, who created the heavens and the earth in six days' (sura 10 v 3). The teaching of the Qur'an on the nature of God's creation is virtually the same as that of the Biblical book of Genesis, therefore, Muslims have many of the same problems regarding evolution as fundamentalist Christians and Jews. Though some western Muslims do try to deal with this, (see *The Bible, the Qur'an and Science*, Maurice Bucaille).

So the Qur'an and Muslims are quite clear that God is creator, this is an essential part of his unity. Indeed the first revelation to Muhammad said, 'Recite in the name of thy Lord who created' (sura 96 v 1).

The Power of God

Clearly if there is only one God who created all that is, he must have complete power over what he has created. Muslims believe that God is 'All-powerful', 'the Absolute'. It is the basis of Islam that you submit to God's will because God is far greater and more powerful than you. This can be seen in the phrase *Allahu Akbar* (God is most great) which is chanted repeatedly during Salah and on many other occasions. As sura 67 v.1 says, 'Blessed be He in whose hands is dominion; and He over all things hath power.'

Muslim beliefs in the power of God can be sub-divided:-

1   God is self-subsistent - he is not dependent on anything else;

2   God is omnipotent - all-powerful, in control of everything that happens;

3   God has a plan for the world and the power to make that plan happen;

4   God is omniscient - knows everything past, present and future;

5   God can change what is going to happen;

6   God is infinite, not only does He have no beginning and no end, but he contains the possibility of all things in Himself.

Clearly the power of God has implications for human freedom which will be dealt with in al'Qad'r.

God's Control of the End of the World

If God is one, the creator and the all-powerful, it follows, to Muslims, that he is the one who will bring the world to an end and he is the one who will judge human beings and determine what their final destiny should be. As sura 1 says, God is 'Master of the Day of Judgement.'

This teaching is in a sense part of tawhid but it will be dealt with more fully in the section on akirah.

God's Immanence

So far tawhid has emphasised the transcendence of God i.e. that he is far, far greater than us and is far away from us. This is definitely a major part of Muslim belief in God, but there are elements in the Qur'an, which have been taken up by the *Sufis*, which emphasise how close to us God is, 'We are nearer to man than his jugular vein'(sura 50 v 16).

This is part of what is meant by immanence, but the main concept is that God is part of the universe He has created, 'Withersoever ye turn there is the presence of God' (sura 2 v 115). Therefore, science and learning will be a discovery of God.

This is the great mystery of God in the Qur'an - he is both transcendent and immanent. 'Yet God is also immanent in the light of His transcendence... that is why the Prophet taught that the highest form of tawhid is to see God before, in, and after all things.' (Seyyed Hossein Nasr)

The Mercy and Compassion of God

Every sura except sura 9 begins with reference to the mercy and compassion of God, but this is not something that can be worked out from God's unity, it can only be discovered by the revelation of God in the Qur'an.

The teaching of the Qur'an about humans is that God created Adam to be his vice-regent on earth, 'Thy Lord said to the angels, "I will create a viceregent on earth"... and He taught Adam the nature of all things.' (sura 2 v 30) In other words, Muslims believe that humans are on earth to rule the earth on God's behalf and make the earth the sort of place God wants it to be. Clearly the previous teachings on God's nature make it possible for him to do that, but if he just created humans and then left them to it, he would not be a very compassionate God.

Muslim teaching about God's mercy is that God did not leave humans alone, he sent prophets with his word to show them how to be his vice-regents. Therefore, the fact that God is compassionate and merciful leads naturally into the belief in risalah.

There is another teaching about God's mercy in the Qur'an, namely that if people are not perfect and fail in their attempt to be vice-regents, God will be merciful, under certain conditions, 'With My punishment I visit whom I will; but My mercy extendeth to all things. That mercy I shall ordain for those who do right, and practise regular charity and those who believe in Our signs.'(sura 7 v 156)

Many Muslims take this to mean that God will be merciful and forgive Muslims who try their best, but commit sins. This is an extra reason for going on Hajj to confess your sins at Arafat because this is the Mount of God's mercy.

The Ninety-nine Names of God

'To Him belong the most beautiful names'(sura 59 v 24) led Muslim theologians to search for the names of God in the Qur'an. These names can be recognised in any translation by 'the' followed by a capital letter e.g.'the Self-sufficient Besought of all'.

There are 99 of these names and they sum up the nature of God. Many Muslims use the rosary of 33 beads to remember and recite God's names.

As far as Muslim scholars are concerned, these names are not God's essence (only Allah describes the nature of God), they simply describe the qualities of God. According to the Hadith, Muhammad instructed his followers to meditate on the 99 names rather than the 'Divine Essence'. Certainly many Muslims feel that by meditating on the names, they come closer to God.

General Muslim Beliefs about God's Nature

All Muslims accept that the Qur'an has revealed to them what God is like - the one God who has created everything that is out of nothing. He has no beginning and no end, and is self-subsistent depending on no one for his existence for he has always existed. He is 'the All-powerful' so there are no limits on his presence and he can be with many people at the same time in many different places.

A problem for Muslim theologians has been that these ideas are expressed in the Qur'an in poetic language which tends to describe God's characteristics in human physical terms e.g. that God sees or hears things. In the early days some Muslims claimed that this must mean God has eyes, ears etc. because the Qur'an is literally true. Some theologians, known as Mu'tazilites, rejected this and said that the fact that God is the eternal means he is purely spiritual with no human characteristics. It is impossible for humans to see God because God will always be beyond human comprehension. This led to much debate and the most common modern view (which comes from a ninth-century theologian called al'Ashari) is that God has non-material ears, eyes etc.

and that it will be possible for faithful Muslims to come face to face with God at the Last Day.

This debate on the physical characteristics of God is still going on (especially among Sufis), but for most Muslims the ideas that matter are the characteristics outlined above which are all thought of as being part of God's unity.

Implications of Tawhid

The essential Muslim belief in the oneness of God also means a belief in the oneness of creation. All has been made by the one God and so there must be a unity in creation.

Part of the Muslim concept of vice-regency is that the life of a Muslim must be to seek and then put into operation the unity of creation. This is what lies behind the concept of the *umma* (religious community). There can only be one community and one law because the earth was created a unity.

For these reasons, Muslim theologians teach that a Muslim should seek the oneness of humanity and the oneness of humanity with nature in order to express faith in the oneness of God

2. Risalah

For Muslims, the unity and greatness of God mean that he cannot communicate directly with humans, and yet his mercy and compassion mean that he cannot just leave them to make a mess of their lives. According to the Qur'an, God appointed Adam as a vice-regent and all humans are now God's vice-regents on earth. This means that, as far as Muslims are concerned, people have the responsibility of caring for the earth in the way God wants. Clearly, they cannot do this if they do not know what God wants them to do, therefore God had to find a way of communicating his will to humans.

Angels

According to the Qur'an, angels were God's first creation. They are immortal and do nothing against the will of God. Unlike humans, angels do not have freewill, 'Glory to thee: of knowledge we have none, save what Thou hast taught us.' (sura 2 v 32) Consequently, they are without sin and so are able to enter the presence of God, but they are not as holy as God therefore they are able to communicate with man.

The implication of the Qur'an is that angels are male, 'Those who believe not in the hereafter, name the angels with female names.' (sura 53 v 27) They are also described as having wings, 'who made the angels messengers with wings two, or three, or four' (sura 35 v 1).

The angels praise God in heaven and are the guardians of hell, 'We have none but angels as guardians of the fire' (sura 74 v 31).

The nature of man in relation to the angels is shown by this Hadith,

> God created angels from intellect without sensuality, the beasts from sensuality without intellect, and mankind from both intellect and sensuality. So when a person's intellect overcomes his sensuality, he is better than the angels; but when his sensuality overcomes his intellect, he is worse than the beasts.

Muslim tradition has added to what the Qur'an says, but is based on the Qur'an. So the functions of angels in the Qur'an are headed by a chief angel *Jibrail* who is responsible for giving God's messages to the prophets; *Mikail* looks after heaven and keeps the Devil out of heaven; *Israfil* is responsible for the Day of Judgement and will sound the Last Trumpet; *Izrail* is responsible for taking the final breath from humans when they die.

There are also recording angels who note everything humans do for the book that each of them must read out on the Last Day, and guardian angels who make sure that faithful Muslims are not attacked by the Devil.

According to Muslim tradition angels are made of light and are without sex.

The Devil (*Iblis* or *Shaytan*) was an angel in the Qur'an, he refused to bow down to Adam and so was thrown out of heaven and set up his own kingdom of hell, and he and his evil spirits are made of fire rather than light. Iblis begged God to put off his punishment and God agreed to do so until the Last Day. This is why Iblis is able to tempt humans to go against God. (sura 7 v 11 - 18)

Just as in Christianity and Judaism there is confusion in Islam over the nature of the Devil because if he has any control of either earth or hell, then that implies God is not omnipotent. The generally accepted

Muslim view is that God allows the Devil to tempt us on Earth, but on the Last Day the Devil will also be handed over to the angels of hell for eternal punishment

The Prophets of God

Twenty five prophets are named in the Qur'an, though Muslim tradition says there have been 124,000 !

The main teaching of the Qur'an concerning the prophets is that they bring God's message so that people know how to behave, 'To every people was sent an Apostle: when their Apostle comes before them the matter will be judged between them with justice and they will not be wronged' (sura 10 v 47).

According to Islam, these messengers are not angels, they are humans. They receive the message from an angel but they themselves are human, 'Their Apostles said to them,"True we are human like yourselves"' (sura 14 v 11). All the prophets except Isa were married and had children. However, it is the belief of Muslims that the prophets were sinless once they were called by God and that they should be blessed when their name is mentioned (this is why Muslim authors put PBUH, *peace be upon him,* after a prophet's name).

According to the Qur'an, each prophet was given God's word for their generation (therefore each prophet brought Islam), but their words were either ignored, forgotten or distorted so that God had to send a new prophet with the original message.

The major prophets are:-

Adam - Created as God's vice-regent, Adam fell from grace by giving in to the temptations of the Devil. He was expelled from the Garden of Eden by a whirlwind and came to his senses on Arafat where he confessed his sin, was forgiven by God and became the first prophet. Muslims believe he built the first Ka'ba in Mecca which was subsequently destroyed in the Flood. Adam and Eve had two sons one of whom murdered the other.

Ibrahim - There were several prophets between Adam and *Ibrahim* (Abraham) including *Nuh* (Noah), but for Islam, Ibrahim is regarded as the greatest of the prophets before Isa.

Ibrahim was born to a polytheistic family (showing how the message of the previous prophets had been distorted), but he rejected polytheism and became a Muslim , 'Abraham was not a Jew nor yet a

Christian; but he was true in faith, and bowed his will to God's which is Islam.' (sura 3 v 67)

Ibrahim had two sons who were both prophets, *Ismail* and *Ishaq*. Ismail was the elder son and was born to Hagar. When Ishaq was born, Sarah made Ibrahim take Hagar and Ismail into Arabia. There Ibrahim rebuilt the Ka'ba with the help of Ismail and in Mina he was tested to sacrifice his son. Ibrahim was also tempted by the Devil and threw stones at him. There is a tradition that Ibrahim had a holy book revealed to him, *The Scrolls of Ibrahim*, the name of a book mentioned in the Qur'an.

Muslims believe that Ismail was the prophet of the Arabs and Ishaq was the prophet of the Jews.

Musa - The work of Ibrahim was forgotten and his holy book lost so that a new prophet had to be sent. Musa was born a Jew but brought up by Pharaoh's daughter. He killed an Egyptian and fled to Midian where God called him to lead the Jews out of slavery in Egypt and into God's promised land. He was given the word of God in the Tawrat (Torah), but the people often rejected and distorted his message.

Dawud - The great King of Israel made Jerusalem a holy place for Muslims. He was given the word of God again in the Zabur because of the distortion of the Tawrat, but it was not written down until long after his death so that it was never properly recorded. The only direct quotation from the Bible in the Qur'an comes from the Zabur, 'Before this We wrote in the Psalms, after the message given to Moses: "My servants the righteous shall inherit the earth."'(sura 21 v 105) and (Psalm 37 v 29)

Isa - Isa and his mother *Maryam* are probably the most prominent figures in the Qur'an other than Muhammad. Sura 19 is all about them. According to the Qur'an, Isa was born to a virgin. His mother never had sex and was 'the most virtuous of women' who conceived Isa by the power of God. Isa was given the Holy Book, Injil (Gospel), and performed many miracles (the Qur'an mentions healing lepers, making the dumb speak, the lame walk, raising the dead and making clay birds fly). The Jewish authorities wanted to crucify him, but God would not allow it to happen, 'They said in boast,"We killed Christ Jesus the son of Mary, the Apostle of God"; but they killed him not, nor crucified him, but so it was made to appear to them.' (sura 4 v 157)

Muslims believe that Jesus did not die but was taken up by God to heaven, 'God said, "O Jesus I will take thee and raise thee to Myself and clear thee of the falsehoods of those who blaspheme."' (sura 3 v

55) As a result of this verse and what follows it, Muslim tradition asserts that Isa will return before the end of the world and gather all true Muslims together.

The Qur'an is quite clear that Isa was only a prophet, 'Christ the Son of Mary was no more than an Apostle; many were the apostles that passed away before him. His mother was a woman of truth. They both had to eat their daily food.' (sura 5 v 78)

Muhammad the Seal of the Prophets

The Qur'an does not show Muhammad as being any different from the earlier prophets. He was not an angel or the son of God, he was simply the Messenger of God, 'Muhammad is no more than an Apostle: many were the apostles that passed away before him.'(sura 3 v 144) 'Say,"I am no bringer of new fangled doctrine among the apostles, nor do I know what will be done with me or with you. I follow but that which is revealed to me by inspiration; I am but a Warner open and clear."' (sura 46 v 9)

Unlike Isa, Muhammad performed no miracles, he died an ordinary death and he was buried. He was an ordinary man, but he brought the Qur'an, the greatest miracle of all time. Muslims believe it is God's final word to humanity, given to Muhammad in such a form that it could never be distorted.

It is this that makes Muhammad so important. The way in which he was given the Qur'an, means that it can never be distorted, therefore there can be no more prophets. 'Muhammad is not the father of any of your men, but he is the Apostle of God and the Seal of the Prophets.' (sura 33 v 40)

This is the key to Muslim understanding of risalah. God sent many prophets to men to help them to be good Muslims, but their message had either been distorted or forgotten. Even those who had been given God's holy books had not had them written down immediately, then they were translated and so they lost many of their original features. So, Muslims believe that the Bible contains parts of the Tawrat, Zabur and Injil, but not sufficient for people to read them and know what to do to serve God.

This is what makes Muhammad 'the Seal of the Prophets'. The Qur'an was given to Muhammad by God in Arabic, and it was immediately written down in Arabic, so there are now no differences between copies of the Qur'an. They are the word of God which is why they all have exactly the same Arabic letters. By contrast, Muslims point out that the Bible has lots of differences - it is in different languages and Jewish and Christian scholars do not always agree on what the text should be.

Remember, Islam did not begin with Muhammad. Muslims believe it began with Adam and has always been the same message. In the past God had to send new messengers because the message of Islam had been either lost, ignored or distorted. However, it follows automatically that if the Qur'an is the word of God, delivered in such a way that it can never be distorted, then there will be no need for any more prophets.

Muhammad is therefore 'the Seal of the Prophets' i.e. he acts like the seal people used to put at the end of their letters to prove it had come from them and to make sure that nothing could be added. For Muslims, the Qur'an proves that Muhammad was God's messenger and it can never have any additions. So Muhammad has restored Islam to what God wants it to be, and Muslims believe it can never again go wrong.

This belief in Muhammad being 'the Seal of the Prophets' has many implications for Muslims:

1   As there will be no more prophets, it must follow that Muhammad is the last prophet, so his example must be the final example of how to live your life. This is why the Sunna and Hadith of the Prophet are so important. Muhammad gave Muslims the perfect example of how to live, 'Ye have indeed in the Apostle of God a beautiful pattern of conduct'(sura 33 v 21), so Muslims must find out as much as they can about how he lived and follow his example e.g. Muhammad did not shave so all Muslim men should have beards.

2   Anyone who claims to have a new message, or to be on a par with the Prophet cannot be a Muslim. This causes problems for Shi'as (see chapter seven).

3   There can be no new beliefs other than wnat is in the Qur'an. This can cause problems for re-interpreting in the light of the modern world e.g. the status of women.

4   Point 1 can cause problems for Muslims, because when they start thinking of Muhammad as the perfect example, they are following Muhammad rather than the Qur'an which is wrong. There is always a danger in Islam of thinking that Muhammad was more than a man, but that is shirk.

The teaching of Islam is that all prophets should be regarded with equal respect. When the name of any prophet is mentioned, the words 'peace be upon him ', should be said. All prophets brought the same message of Islam, but there have only been four who were given holy books, and of these only Muhammad was given the book in its final unalterable form, and so there can be no new religions or any additions to Islam. The doctrine of Muhammad, 'the Seal of the Prophets', means that, for Muslims, Islam is the final and ultimate religion.

> The only source, therefore, for the knowledge of God and His Way is Muhammad (blessings of Allah and peace be upon him). We can know of Islam only through his teachings which are so complete and so comprehensive that they can guide men through all ages to come. (Abul Ala Mawdudi)

Holy Books

Muslim teaching on holy books is to be found in the chapter on the Qur'an (chapter one).

3. Akirah

The Nature of Humanity

According to the teachings of Islam on humans as God's vice-regents, humans are thinking rational creatures whose duty is to follow the faith of Islam and so make this world the sort of place God wants it to be. God has given the Qur'an and the Sunna of Muhammad to show them what to do, and it is up to them to follow these. If they do not, then they will,only have themselves to blame when God punishes them on the Last Day.

It is a fundamental belief of Islam that this life is not all there is. This life is simply a preparation (some Muslims would say a test) for the life to come, 'Be sure We shall test you with something of fear and hunger, some loss in goods or lives or the fruits of your toil, but give glad tidings to those who patiently persevere' (sura 2 v 155). The sort of life Muslims lead in the world to come will depend on how they have performed as God's vice-regents in this life.

The Last Day in the Qur'an

The Qur'an teaches resurrection of the dead rather than immortality of the soul i.e. when you die your soul does not go straight to heaven, instead it waits in the grave until the Last Day when soul and body will be rejoined and the raised person will come out of the grave. 'They say, "What! When we are reduced to bones and dust should we really be raised up to be a new creation? ... Who will cause us to return?" Say, "He who created you first."' (sura 17 v 49 -51)

On the day itself the world as we know it will disappear , 'On the Day when the firmament will be in dreadful commotion and the mountains will fly hither and thither.' (sura 52 v 9,10)

According to the Qur'an, the Last Day will be heralded by the sound of a trumpet, everything will stop, then heaven and earth will change and the raised dead will join the living.

> On the Day of Judgement, the whole of the earth will be but His handful and the heavens will be rolled up in His right hand... The Trumpet will be sounded when all that are in the heavens and the earth will swoon (lose consciousness) except such as it will please God to exempt. Then will a second one be sounded, when, behold, they will be standing and looking on! And the earth will shine with the glory of its Lord. (sura 39 v 67 - 69)

The Qur'an states that no one knows when the Last Day will be except God (sura 33 v 63, sura 57 v 26, sura 79 v 42 - 46).

The Last Day and Muslim Tradition

The period between individual death and the final judgement is known as *Barzakh*, and there are many different beliefs about its nature.

Some Muslim traditions say that when you die, you are visited by the angel of death, Izrail, who will question you about your faith. If you answer with the Shahada, you will be shown your place in heaven, but if you answer wrongly, you will be beaten with clubs until the Last Day. Other Muslim traditions say that your body dies and your soul hovers over the grave until the Last Day. Whereas others claim that your soul simply sleeps until the Last Day, so that it will only seem like a moment between death and resurrection.

As to the signs of the end, some Muslim traditions assert that the world will become evil as it is taken over by *Dajjal*. Isa will then return to the

Damascus Mosque and lead the faithful out against Dajjal and defeat him. Then the Trumpet will sound. Other Muslim traditions claim that the *Mahdi* will appear and convert the world to Islam before Israfil sounds the Trumpet.

Islam has millenarians (people who believe that the end will come before the year 2000) who read the Hadith about the end of the world and deduce from them that Dajjal will soon appear, 'Many of the signs of the end of the world are clearly indicated in the Hadith collections... all the signs of the end of the world are now apparent except for the last four major signs, and it would appear that even these are now imminent...' (*Dajjal The King who has no clothes*, Ahmad Thomson)

However, most Muslims accept the teachings of the Qur'an that no one knows when the end will be.

Judgement in the Qur'an

The Qur'an says that the dead and the living will be raised and brought to the plain of judgement. There they will stand naked before God. Each person will be given the book of their life to read out to everyone there and to God (this is the record kept by the recording angels). Those given the book in their right hand will go to heaven and those given the book in their left hand will go to hell. Everything a person has ever done will be in the book, and he or she will have to read out his or her deepest secrets.

The basis of judgement seems to be a mixture of faith and action,

> That Day shall all men be sorted out. Then those who have believed and worked righteous deeds shall be made happy in a mead of delight. And those who have rejected faith and falsely denied our signs and the meeting of the Hereafter - such shall be brought forth to punishment. (sura 30 v 14 - 16)

There are other verses which imply that only good Muslims will pass the judgement and this is the normally accepted Muslim belief about judgement - that good Muslims will pass the judgement but non-Muslims and bad Muslims will fail and be sent to hell.

Other Views on Judgement

Verses such as, 'Whoever does evil will be requited accordingly nor will he find, besides God, any protector or helper,' (sura 4 v 123), lead many Muslims to believe that God will intercede for Muslims who have tried their best, but committed sins. After all, God is 'the Merciful,' 'the Compassionate,' and he will surely show mercy on the Last Day.

After-life in the Qur'an

The Qur'an paints very vivid pictures of heaven and hell.

Heaven is *al'Jannah* (the Garden) with streams and rivers, flowers and plants. It is a place where the blessed will have all their hearts desires. They will recline on couches, eat the choicest fruits and drink wine which delights but does not intoxicate.

Hell is *Jahannan* (the place of fire) and is a place of horrors. The inhabitants are chained up, given boiling water and puss to drink and garments of fire to wear. Boiling water is poured over their heads and when their skins are too burnt to feel the pain, then new skins will be given to them.

The fullest description of heaven and hell can be found in sura 56 v 1 - 56. This concrete description of heaven and hell is very similar to that in the New Testament, especially the book of Revelation.

The implication of the Qur'an is that whether you go to heaven or hell you will stay there for ever , 'Companions of the Fire... will abide therein for ever.' (sura 2 v 275)

After-life in Later Muslim Thought

The vast majority of Muslims accept the teachings of the Qur'an as they are traditionally interpreted and so believe that after judgement you go to heaven or hell and stay there for ever.

Some Muslim scholars, however, see the descriptions in the Qur'an as metaphorical rather than literal, 'God explains the Garden in terms of houris, castles, trees and rivers in order that it may be understood in these terms. But in fact, how should the Garden resemble such things? For they are transitory, while it is eternal.' (Sultan Walad)

Some Muslim scholars also take certain verses and use them to justify a slightly different position. Sura 15 v 44 says of Hell, 'To it are seven gates: for each of those gates is a special class of sinners assigned.' Sura 6 v 128 says, 'The Fire be your dwelling place: you will dwell therein for ever except as God willeth.' Some modernist Muslims use these verses to claim that maybe only the very worst will stay in hell for ever and that bad Muslims and good Jews and Christians will only be in hell for a short period.

A very few westernised Muslims (and some Sufis) use the belief that Muslims who die on Hajj or on Jihad will go straight to heaven, to argue that the after-life is therefore spiritual. For them the Qur'an is allegorical on the Last Things, your soul is judged when you die and then goes to a spiritual heaven or hell (for the Sufi view see the chapter on 'Eschatology' in *Islamic Spirituality Foundations*). However, it must be emphasised that very few such Muslims hold these beliefs.

The Implications of Akirah

The major implication of belief in akirah is that Muslims must live the whole of their lives aware that everything they do is being noted down and they will be judged on it by God on the Last Day.

This means a Muslim should be concerned all the time about whether he/she is living their life in the way God wants them to. Part of the belief in akirah is the belief that Islam is a way of life, it is not just a religion. Having religiously submitted to the will of God, a Muslim must live the whole of their life submitted to God.

Akirah means that for a Muslim the whole of life is *ibadah* (worship). A Muslim follows the Five Pillars and the Shari'a, not only because they are a Muslim, but also because they know that they will be judged on how far their life has revealed submission and that the nature of their after-life depends on that judgement.

> If you reflect still deeper, you will come to the conclusion that belief in life after death is the most decisive factor in the life of a man... A man who has in view success or failure in this world alone... will not be prepared to undertake any good act... nor will he be keen to avoid any wrong act... But a man who believes in the next world as well... will do the good... and he will avoid the wrong... He will judge things from the viewpoint of their eternal consequences. (Abul Ala Mawdudi)

4. Al Qad'r

Al Qad'r means that everything in the universe is following a divine masterplan, ' The command of God is a decree determined.' (sura 33 v 38). 'In all things the master-planning is God's.' (sura 13 v 42).

This is, of course, a simple conclusion from the Muslim belief in tawhid. Throughout the Qur'an there are references to the way in which things happened in the lives of the prophets which they did not understand at the time, but later came to see as part of God's plan for their lives. As Yusuf says at the end of sura 12,

> This is the fulfilment of my vision of old! God hath made it come true! He was indeed good to me when He took me out of prison and brought you out of the desert, even after Satan had sown emnity between me and my brothers. Verily my Lord understandeth best the mysteries of all He planneth to do.

However, if God has a master plan for the universe, if God is all-powerful and nothing happens without God's permission, does not that mean that God is responsible for evil ? Clearly one Muslim answer to this question is provided by the belief in akirah. If God is going to judge us on the basis of our actions and punish us for them, it must follow that we have free will. No law court would ever judge someone and punish them if they were not responsible for their actions.

This was the line taken by the eighth-century Muslim theologians known as the Mu'tazilites. They claimed that God created humans with free will as his vice-regents and it is therefore up to humans what happens in the world. They then took this to its logical conclusion and denied the very idea of al Qad'r. This caused the more orthodox eighth-century Muslim theologian al'Ashari to develop an idea which combines free will and al Qad'r - God knows what people will do before they do it, but it is up to their free will to decide whether to do what God wants or not. God has the quality of foreknowledge (sifat) - he knows what people will do, but they do it of our own free will.

> God's will reigns supreme in a universe in which His power dominates over all things and all human actions... Yet in such a world man is mysteriously endowed with the gift of freedom of action, which holds him responsible before God for whatever action he commits. (Seyyed Hossein Nasr)

Many Muslims in the Middle Ages ignored the teachings of both these groups of theologians and began to take al Qad'r and the concept of *insh Allah* (if God wills) to mean that humans have no free will and that God controls directly everything that happens.

Nowadays the more conventional Muslim view is that expressed by Ghulam Sarwar,

> By believing in al Qad'r we testify that God is the Absolute Controller of the affairs of His universe. It is He who decides what is good and what is bad... We are unable to understand and interpret many of Allah's actions. It is meaningless to argue that human beings act without freedom and that we are forced to act the way we do. We decide for ourselves what we will do, and what we will not, and we are responsible for our own actions. This freedom of action does not conflict with the foreknowledge of Allah.

So Muslims believe that God has a plan for the universe he has created; that he has the power to make that plan happen (he is omnipotent) and that he knows what will happen (he is omniscient - sifat) so that in the end all will work out as God wants. If we cannot understand how this can fit in with human free will, this is because we are far from being like God and therefore we cannot expect to understand all of God's ways.

CHAPTER THREE

THE FIVE PILLARS OF ISLAM

Worship

As far as most Muslims are concerned Islam is a way of life. It is not a religious belief which you can shut off from your ordinary day-to-day life. Worship is not a matter of occasionally remembering God or even going to the mosque five times a day, it is an attitude to life, 'Worship, according to Islam , is a means for the purification of man's soul and his practical life.' (Mustafa Ahmad al'Zarqa)

If you have accepted the Six Beliefs of Islam and decided to submit yourself to the will of God, you are a Muslim and Muslims worship God in the whole of their lives. Eating, drinking, marriage, all come under the scope of worship if a Muslim is performing them with the right attitude. 'It is because of this basis that Muslim jurists and scholars have proclaimed that good intention changes acts of habit (adah) into acts of worship (ibadah).' (Mustafa Ahmad al'Zarqa) 'Everything we do comes under ibadah, if we do it for Allah's sake. Our purpose in life is to please Allah through ibadah.' (Ghulam Sarwar)

This fact of Islam is seen in the way in which many Muslims refer to the 'House of Islam'. Just as you live much of your life in your house so Muslims can live their whole life in the House of Islam.

A house has foundations and for Islam this is the Qur'an. The way a Muslim should worship, and therefore everything a Muslim has to do, is based on the Qur'an. This is the Word of God, it is the basis of Islam and so it is the foundation of faith and worship.

In the Middle East every house was supported on pillars. The support of the House of Islam is the 'Five Pillars' of witness, prayer, charity, fasting and pilgrimage.

> On the authority of Abu Abd ar'Rahman Abdullah, the son of Umar ibn al'Khattab who said,'I heard the messenger of Allah say, "Islam has been built on five pillars: testifying that there is no god but Allah and that Muhammad is the Messenger of Allah, performing the prayers, paying the zakat, making pilgrimage to

the House and fasting in Ramadan."' (Hadith quoted by Bukhari and Muslim)

All houses also need a roof and for the House of Islam the roof is the Holy Law (Shari'a).

A Muslim is someone who has submitted to the will of God as revealed in the Holy Qur'an to the Prophet Muhammad. But Islam can never be theoretical, it is always practical. If you have submitted to the will of God, then there must be practical signs of that submission. Those practical signs are the pillars. The pillars cut off a Muslim from a non-Muslim, and they show that the person peforming them is one who has submitted to the will of God and who is worshipping God through them.

1. Shahada

This is the central pillar even though it is the only 'non-action' pillar. Iman (faith) provides the central pillar that sustains the whole structure. (Kurshid Ahmad)

This central pillar is, *La ilaha illal lahu. Muhammadur rasulul la* - There is no god but God. Muhammad is the Prophet of God.

These are the words of the Shahada, the Muslim creed. They sum up all you have to believe to be a Muslim - the unity of God and the prophethood of Muhammad. From these two simple beliefs all the other beliefs are derived - the unity of creation and humanity, the vice-regency of humans, angels, prophets, holy books. If you accept Muhammad as the prophet of God, then you accept the Qur'an as the word of God and the Sunna of Muhammad as the path to follow. That is why if someone converts to Islam, all they have to do to show their conversion is repeat the shahada in front of witnesses. 'A man joins the fold of Islam by honestly believing in and professing faith in the unity of God and the prophethood of Muhammad.' (Kurshid Ahmad)

There are no ceremonies in Islam which make you a Muslim. All you need do is declare the words of the Shahada, and then you are recognised as a Muslim.

A Muslim, and especially a Muslim convert, will know fom the Shahada that Islam rejects both polytheism and trinitarianism. There is no god but God. The Shahada reminds Muslims that there is no way that Muhammad can be regarded on a par with God. Islam is nothing like Christianity, where Jesus is regarded as God, for Muhammad is only a prophet.

The words of the Shahada are repeated many times a day in the prayer ritual. They are announced five times a day from the *minaret* of the mosque. Muslim fathers are expected to whisper the words into the ear of their newborn child so that they are the first words the child hears, and faithful Muslims, who know they are about to die, try to make these words their last breath. Muslim soldiers go into battle with these words always on their lips.

This is why the Shahada is the first pillar because all the rest are simply an outward expression of its meaning which is why the other four pillars are signs of ibadah.

2. Salah

The Qur'an says, 'Set up Regular Prayers; for such prayers are enjoined on believers at stated times.' (sura 4 v 103)

There are many other such verses in the Qur'an about how Muslims must pray, how they should prepare themselves for prayer and the benefits of prayer.

Salah is one of those pillars which shows most clearly the relationship between Qur'an and Sunna. The Qur'an says that you must pray at fixed times, but it is unclear as to exactly what those fixed times are, 'Establish regular prayers at the sun's decline till the darkness of the night, and the morning prayer and reading for the prayer and reading in the morning carry their testimony. And pray in the small watches of the morning an additional prayer.' (sura 17 v 78) Therefore, Muslims follow the example of how the Prophet prayed (Sunna). So the ritual prayer of Salah is based on a mixture of what the Qur'an says and how the Prophet Muhammad actually carried out the ritual.

Salah is regarded by Muslim scholars as the most important of the practical pillars, 'the prayers and all other prescribed forms of worship for that matter, serve to distinguish those who do really have faith and wish sincerely to serve God from those who are content with lip-service.' (Mustafa Ahmad al'Zarqa)

Indeed, according to a Hadith, Muhammad said, 'Salah is the pillar of the Islamic religion and whoever abandons it, demolishes the very pillar of religion.'

The Prayer Ritual

1   The times for prayer are:

> *Fajr* (between dawn and sunrise)
>
> *Zuhr* (after mid-day until afternoon)
>
> *As'r* (between late afternoon and sunset)
>
> *Maghrib* (between sunset and end of daylight)
>
> *Isha* (between sunset and dawn)

All mosques have a board with six clocks on showing the times of prayer for a week plus the the time of *Juma* (Friday) prayers. Obviously, the times of prayer vary from week to week everywhere, except the equator, because of the time of sunrise and sunset.

2   The time of prayer should be announced by a *muezzin* who calls out the *adhan* (call to prayer) from the minaret,

> Allah is the greatest *(Allahu akbar)* - (four times)
>
> I bear witness that there is no god but God, and   Muhammad is the Prophet of God - (four times)
>
> Rush to prayer - (twice)
>
> Rush to success - (twice)
>
> Allah is greatest - (twice)
>
> There is no god but God - (once)

At *Fajr* prayers 'Salah is better than sleep' is called twice after 'rush to success'.

3   Then the faithful Muslims should respond to the call of the muezzin by preparing for prayer. This means that they must perform *wudu*.

Prayer is the most sacred moment of life, for it is when a Muslim comes into direct contact with God. The Islamic beliefs about God mean that this can never be done in an ordinary fashion and so a Muslim must prepare through the ritual washing ceremony (hands, arms, face, feet, nostrils, ears, and head each washed three times in running water. At certain times a complete bath - *ghusl* -

is required, but this can never be done in the presence of anyone else (as Muslims must never be seen naked) and by wearing clean clothes (a very pious Muslim will change their underwear five times a day).

If a Muslim is not praying in the mosque, an essential feature of wudu is to make sure there is a clean place on which to pray. This is why many Muslims on a journey will carry a prayer mat with them which has never been trodden on by anything unclean. Many Muslims have a special room in the house which will never be entered whilst wearing outdoor shoes so that it is clean for Salah.

This is why, if you visit a mosque, you will have to remove your shoes before entering the prayer hall so that it is always clean for prayer.

4   It is preferable for prayers to be said in the mosque, 'bow down your heads with those who bow down in worship.' (sura 2 v 43), but prayers can be said anywhere as long as all the right conditions are fulfilled.

5   Next, a Muslim must have the correct *qibla* (direction of prayer). Prayers must be said facing Mecca (actually the Ka'ba). This is easy in the mosque because there is always a *mihrab* (niche) in the wall to show the qibla. However, away from the mosque it is much more difficult which is why many prayer mats have a qibla compass for the worshipper to find Mecca.

6   Now the Muslim must make the *iqama* (the call to prayer just before prayer begins). This is the same as the adhan except it has 'The salah has begun' added before the final *takbir* (God is the greatest).

If praying in the mosque, this will be said by the *imam* (prayer leader).

7   Each prayer time consists of a set number of *raka't* - this is the prayer ritual - the main features of which are:

a) make your *niyya* (prayer of intention - saying why you are praying - intended to stop Salah becoming a meaningless ritual);

b) whilst standing with hands to ears, then arms folded, you praise God with some set prayers and recite sura 1, *al'fatiha* (you can follow this with some other verses from the Qur'an praising God);

c) then kneel on the floor and touch your forehead on the ground without your arms touching the ground. (This is called *sujud* and is an outward sign of your inner submission.);

d) you then raise the top half of your body but stay on your knees whilst giving God the glory, then you prostrate yourself again;

e) you then stand up saying God is the greatest.

This completes one *raka*, and you now start again. However, once during each Salah you must say:

tashahhud - a prayer requesting peace and blessings from God on the people around you and ending with reptition of the Shahada;

darud - a prayer requesting blessings for Muhammad and the prophets of God.

These come at different times depending on how many raka't there are in the Salah.

8   Now a Muslim may make their own prayers to God (these are called *Du'a* and are not an essential part of Salah - though they are regarded as such by some law schools).

9   When they have finished all their raka't and Du'a Muslims must end their Salah with '*Assalamu alaikum wa rahmatullah*' (the peace and mercy of Allah be upon you) said over your right and then left shoulders whilst you are still kneeling.

The number of raka't are divided into *fard* (compulsory prayers), *sunna* (optional prayers which Muhammad prayed as extras) and *nafrilla* (totally optional), as shown below:

Fajr - two fard, two sunna

Zuhr - four fard, six sunna

As'r - four fard, four nafrilla

Maghrib - three fard, two sunna

Isha - four fard, four nafrilla, two sunna, and three *witr* (these are also sunna, but are said by many Muslims who do not say the other optional prayers).

If a Muslim cannot say their prayers because of travel or work, it is possible to join together prayers at the next prayer time.

Juma Prayers

Sura 62 v 10 says, 'O ye who believe! When the call is proclaimed to prayer on Friday (the Day of Assembly), hasten earnestly to the remembrance of God, and leave off business: that is best for you if ye but knew! And when the Prayer is finished, then ye may disperse through the land and seek of the bounty of God.'

From this has come the practice of Muslims gathering in the mosques on Friday for the Zuhr prayers.

These prayers have to be attended by at least 40 adult male Muslims and so are held in specially designated mosques called *Jami Mosques* where it is expected that there will be at least 40 worshippers. The imam leads the congregation in the first two raka't of Zuhr prayers and then preaches a sermon (*khutba*) either on how to behave as a Muslim in the particular community where the mosque is situated, or for telling Hadith about the Prophet. It is also used for passing on information to the Muslim community.

In a Muslim state, the Head of State should be the imam of the Juma prayers just as the Prophet was in Medina and the Caliphs were in Baghdad.

There is no official day of rest in Islam and work can recommence after the Juma prayers. Shops etc. only need to close for two hours around lunchtime.

There is a tradition in Asian Islam that women do not have to attend Juma prayers as it might interfere with their household duties, but in many countries they are expected to attend and certainly sura 62 seems to apply to women as much as men.

These are the main prayers connected with Salah, but there are other Salah prayers connected with funerals (*janazah* prayers), the *eids* and *Ramadan* (*tarawih* prayers).

The absolute importance of Salah can be seen from the following Hadith, 'those who offer their Salah with great care and punctuality will find it a light, a proof of their faith and cause of their salvation on the Day of Judgement.'

Du'a Prayers

Prayer is divided into Salah and Du'a, because Salah only takes place at the set times, but the concept of ibadah means that the whole of your life should be a prayer to God. Du'a is therefore the way you can pray to God for forgiveness and remember him at every moment of your life.

Although Du'a prayers are voluntary, some Muslims regard the Du'a prayers at the end of Salah as compulsory.

Du'a prayers can be said in your own language (the whole of Salah must be said in Arabic), but many Muslims learn Du'a prayers in Arabic to recite on such occasions as meals, entering a building, getting on a vehicle, making a decision, going to bed and waking up. These prayers are usually relevant verses from the Qur'an.

The Image of God that comes from Salah

1   God is holy. He is totally different from and separate to humans and so can only be approached by those who have purified themselves from the contamination of daily life by performing wudu.

2   God is 'the All-powerful' to whom people's only response is submission which is why the worshipper must bow to God and prostrate before God as a sign of submission.

    This can also be seen in the words 'Allahu akbar' (God is most great) which must be repeated at least a hundred times a day by a faithful Muslim.

3   God is the guide of Muslims and so at the beginning of Salah a Muslim must put hands to ears to show they are ready to listen to what God tells them to do. This is why they say at least 20 times a day 'I seek shelter in Allah from the rejected Satan' and 'Guide me in the straight path, the path of those whom thou hast blessed'.

4   God is the one and only God. This is seen not so much in what is done, as in what is said in Salah. Firstly the muezzin calls out 15 times a day that there is no god but God. This is then repeated in the iqama. The key words of the *fatiha* (repeated many times in

Salah) are 'You alone we worship, to you alone we pray for help'.

5   God is so great and wonderful, but also compassionate and
     merciful that He deserves our worship and praise. The whole
     ritual is concerned with praising God and these words are
     repeated frequently, 'Oh Allah, glory and praise are for you and
     blessed is Your name and exalted is Your majesty', 'Glory to my
     Lord the great' and 'All prayer is for Allah and worship and
     goodness'.

6   There can be no intermediaries between God and humans. Prayer
     is offered to God alone. In Salah there is no mention of prophets
     until the darud at the very end. Even so some Muslims omit this
     prayer because they feel it is making Islam like Christianity.
     Darud is not said by the Wahhabis of Saudi-Arabia

7   God is 'the Accepter of Prayer', but Salah is not concerned with
     asking God for things, it is concerned with putting humans into
     contact with God, though in Du'a at the end of Salah most
     Muslims will ask God to forgive them their sins.

The Religious Significance of Salah

Many of the points on the image of God show the religious significance
of Salah, but the following points also emerge from consideration of
the religious significance of Salah:

1   For most Muslims the main significance of Salah is that it puts
     them in contact with God five times a day.

     If five times a day he (any person) were to remove himself from
     the corrupting taint of worldly transactions in which he is apt to
     lose himself and were to make an effort consciously to identify
     himself with the pursuit of the supreme goal... and were to seek
     persistently from his Creator the help he needs... then there can
     be no doubt that he would succeed in adhering to the path of
     righteousness. (Allahbakhsh K. Brohi)

2   A Muslim can never forget that they have submitted themselves to
     God's will because Salah is performed five times a day. They
     would also be reminded of all the other implications of their
     submission to God at all times.

3   Salah unites a Muslim with all his fellow Muslims. It is a practical
     expression of the brotherhood of Islam, as they pray in lines

behind the imam all performing the same actions and saying the same words. Salah is a unifying force. ' The ritual prayer, over and above its benefit to the individual, has a social aspect in that it brings one closer to his fellow men and promotes the life of the community by integrating its members into a fraternal feeling of oneness.' (Allahbakhsh K. Brohi)

4   Salah brings an awareness of the fundamentals of the Muslim faith - submission (in the actions etc.) and peace (in the feeling of oneness with God, your fellow Muslims and in the words of peace at the end).

5   Salah is a discipline. The actual physical actions keep a Muslim fit and force Muslims to take their religion seriously.They are a constant reminder of your faith and the fact that your faith means action.

6   Many Muslims believe that if you perform Salah properly and regularly, your sins will be forgiven. As a Hadith says, 'The five prayers remove sins as water removes dirt.'

The importance of Salah can be seen in this comment by Abul Ala Mawdudi,

Can there be a better course of moral and spiritual training than prayers? It is this training that makes a man a perfect Muslim. It reminds him of his covenant with God, refreshes his faith in Him and keeps the belief in the Day of Judgement alive and ever present before his mind's eye. It makes him follow the Prophet and trains him in the observance of his duties.

Salah does provide problems for Muslims living in non-Muslim countries. If they have a job with a non-Muslim firm, they will have to miss some of the prayer times and most probably Friday prayers. The fact that prayer times vary makes it very difficult for employers to accommodate Muslim employees. However, Muslims can use the regulation on joining prayers together and still complete their Salah every day. Some Muslims who do not work on production lines have persuaded their employers to set a room aside for prayers and they take their breaks at prayer times so they can complete them properly.

Other Muslims find the requirements of Salah too burdensome and only do Salah morning and evening (or even more occasionally) and hope to use their retirement to make up all their prayer times. Others just trust in the mercy of Allah to forgive them as long as they have kept the Shari'a and the other four pillars

3. Zakah

Islam teaches that wealth is something given by God for the benefit of humanity and, therefore, it is something to be shared. In Islam, sharing your wealth is not an optional extra, it is compulsory and is an annual tax on wealth. If you are a Muslim, you must perform Zakah as part of your worship (ibadah) of God.

Zakah began in Medina after the first battles when there were widows and orphans who had to be looked after. Sura 2 v 215 says, 'They ask thee, what they should spend in charity. Say,"Whatever ye spend that is good is for parents and kindred and orphans and those in want and for wayfarers. And whatever ye do that is good, God knoweth it well"'.

Zakah is the third pillar because it is closely connected with Salah. In Arabic Zakah means 'purification' and it is possible that one of the ideas behind Zakah is that wealth can be an evil thing and can cut you off from God. Therefore, a Muslim pays Zakah so that the money they have left is pure, it will not contaminate them, and they will be able to perform their Salah without any worries.There is a Hadith which says, 'Protect your property by giving zakat, and help your relatives to recover from disease by giving charity.'

Allahbakhsh K. Brohi says of the connection between Salah and Zakah,

> It would appear that the efficaciousness of the prayer is very much dependent on what man is freely able to give from his wealth in the Name of God. This is not merely a case of performing charity but of securing his purification... It seems as if man is carrying a bone-breaking burden of wealth on his head as he is travelling on his way to God, and he is advised that by giving zakat he would be able to jettison this burden... Both prayer and the giving of zakat are calculated to purify men; it will be recalled that the Prophet was explicitly enjoined to purify the believers, (sura 52 v 2).

Of course, because of what the Qur'an says, Zakah is also a religious duty it is a sign of your submission to God and your worship of Him. You cannot call yourself a Muslim if you do not pay the Zakah.

The major difficulty with Zakah for a Muslim is that the Qur'an does not specify exactly how much you should pay. Sura 2 v 254 says, 'O ye who believe! spend out of the bounties We have provided for you,' and verse 215 says, 'They ask thee what they should spend in charity. Say, "Whatever ye spend, that is good"'.

So in Zakah also the Sunna of the Prophet, the sayings of the Prophet and eventually the decisions of the Law Schools are referred to so that a Muslim can see exactly what to do.

The Qur'an says that there should be a minimum level of living before you are liable to Zakah - clearly the poor cannot be expected to give Zakah. The Law Schools have named this the *nisab*. It varies from occupation to occupation and is quite complex, but in essence is the same as the British tax allowance whereby you are allowed to earn £3,250 before you start paying income tax.

When once you reach the nisab then what you pay as Zakah depends on your job and situation. Agricultural Zakah is 10 per cent of produce in non-irrigated land and 5 per cent on irrigated. Cattle Zakah varies from animal to animal.Traders are expected to pay 2.5 per cent of the value of what they have traded. People with gold, silver, jewellery or cash in the bank have to pay 2.5 per cent of the value if they have had it for 12 months. The position of wage earners is more uncertain especially for Muslims living in the West where there is no *Ulama* (group of Muslim lawyers who decide the laws in a Muslim country). Most Muslims in the UK feel that they must give 2.5 per cent of their income above the nisab, though again it is difficult to find the nisab for a wage earner.

Zakah has to be used to provide for orphans, widows, the poor, the homeless, tax collectors, and religious purposes (e.g. Muslim schools, building new mosques etc.). This is based on sura 9 v 60 'Alms are for the poor and the needy, and those employed to administer the funds; for those whose hearts have been recently reconciled to the truth; for those in bondage and debt; in the cause of God and for the wayfarer.'

There are special Zakahs to be paid on the eids. Muslims feel especially constrained to pay the *eid al'fitr* Zakah because, having fasted during Ramadan, they can sympathise with the starving. *Zakah al'fitr* is currently £1.25 per member of your family. *Zakah al'adha* should be a share in the sacrificed meat for the poor, but often is a donation to Muslim Aid for the Third World starving. Many mosques have a Zakah box so that Muslims can pay their Zakah and then a committee decides what to do with the money.

Clearly, Zakah is a way of ensuring that all Muslims share in the gifts of God, and is a sign of Muslim brotherhood. Many modern Muslim fundamentalists feel that Islam has stopped observing Zakah properly and that is why Muslim countries lag behind the West in welfare provision. They teach that all Muslims, and especially all Muslim states, should enforce Zakah properly to narrow the gap between rich and poor as the Prophet and Qur'an intended, 'Seest thou one who denies the judgement to come ? Then such is the man who repulses the orphan and encourages not the feeding of the indigent.' (sura 107 v 1 - 3)

As Abul Ala Mawdudi said,

> Muslim society has much to gain from the institution of Zakah. It is the bounden duty of every well-to-do Muslim to help his lowly placed poor brethren. His wealth is not to be spent solely for his own comfort and luxury - there are rightful claimants on his wealth, and they are the nation's widows and orphans, the poor and the invalid; those who have the ability but lack the means to gain useful employment and those who have the talent but not the money to acquire knowledge and become useful members of society.

Just as prayer is divided by Muslims into compulsory (Salah) and voluntary (Du'a), so charity is divided into the compulsory Zakah and the voluntary *Sadaqah*. Sadaqah would be what you give a beggar in the street or what you put in a collecting box for something like Oxfam. Muslims often give Sadaqah if they want forgiveness for a sin they have committed or if they want to thank God for something.

4. Sawm

Sawm means fasting and the Qur'an makes it quite plain that to be a Muslim you must practise fasting, 'O ye who believe! Fasting is prescribed to you as it was prescribed to those before you that ye may learn self-restraint, fasting for a fixed number of days; but if any of you is ill or on a journey, the prescribed number should be made up from days later.' (sura 2 v 183 - 4)

> Ramadhan is the month in which was sent down the Qur'an as a guide to mankind, also clear signs for guidance and judgement. So everyone of you who is present at his home in that month should spend it in fasting. But if anyone is ill, or on a journey, the prescribed period should be made up by days later. God intends every facility for you; He does not want to put you to difficulties... Permitted to you on the night of the fasts is the approach to your wives, they are your garments and ye are their

garments... eat and drink until the white thread of dawn appears to you distinct from its black thread; then complete your fast till the night appears; but do not associate with your wives while ye are in retreat in the mosques. Those are limits set by God. (sura 2 v 185 - 190)

From this and other statements in the Qur'an came the belief that fasting is a fourth pillar - a religious duty which Muslims must perform to show their devotion to God.

When must a Muslim fast ?

Although Muslims can fast at any time (except on eid al'fit'r and *eid al'adha*) as a sign of devotion to God, the fard (compulsory) fast soon became the month of Ramadan, and, although the Qur'an only specifies a number of days, it soon became the practice to follow the custom of Muhammad and fast for the whole of the month of Ramadan.

Ramadan had been a traditional holy month in Arabia and fell around mid-summer. It was a truce month and a time when holy men fasted. Muhammad seems to have determined that Muslim religious practices would be rid of any connections with Meccan polytheism and, in particular, with seasons of the year. So he decreed that the Arab calendar would no longer have a thirteenth month every three or four years (which is necessary to keep a lunar calendar in line with the earth's orbit of the sun). So the Muslim year only has 354 days so that 33 Muslim years equal 32 solar ones. Therefore, in 32 years a Muslim month will have occurred in all the seasons of the year. As a result fasting in Ramadan moves back 11 days every year (e.g. if Ramadan begins on 25 March in 1992, it will begin on 23 February in 1993 etc.).

The obligation to fast begins on the first day of Ramadan (which traditionally occurs when one reliable witness convinces the religious authorities that he has seen the new moon). The fast ends when the next new moon is seen. Muslims must fast between the hours of dawn and dusk. The times for fasting in the UK are laid down by the authorities of the Central Mosque in Regent's Park London, though some Muslims phone relatives in their homeland to determine the first and last days of Ramadan.

Who has to fast ?

Everyone over the age of puberty (usually reckoned as 14) must fast - although many children fast voluntarily before this age. The sick and menstruating women are not allowed to fast and people on journeys can be excused.

What do Muslims do when they fast ?

Fasting means no food, drink, smoking, the inhalation of anything other than air through the mouth or nose, and no sexual intercourse. This lasts from dawn to dusk. Therefore, special meals are eaten after dusk and just before dawn (known as *suhur*).

Fasting also means saying not only Salah, but also making extra prayers. Tarawih prayers replace wit'r (the extra night prayer which is not fard) during Ramadan and include recitation of a thirtieth of the Qur'an during Ramadan so that during the month the whole of the Qur'an is recited. This can be done either in the mosque or at home.

All Muslims should try to attend the mosque on *Lailat al'Qad'r* (which is celebrated by most Muslims on the 27 Ramadan) for the tarawih prayer because this is the celebration of the night when Muhammad received his first revelation of the Qur'an and special prayers are said thanking God for the Qur'an.

All Muslims who fast should also refrain from telling lies, gossipping, getting angry with each other, swearing etc. as this is regarded as a part of the fast.

Why do Muslims fast in Ramadan ?

1   Keeping the fast is obeying the fourth pillar and shows the world you are a Muslim.

2   The greatest gift God has given to a Muslim is the Qur'an and Ramadan is a celebration of the gift of the Qur'an to Muslims. It is only right and proper that something should be given up as a sign of your gratefulness to God for this gift.

3   Fasting brings Muslims closer to God, as you can concentrate on God instead of the ordinary things of life.

4   Fasting gives Muslims an opportunity to identify with the poor. Many Muslims feel they can give their eid Zakah from the heart because, having fasted for a month, they sympathise with the plight of the starving.

5   Fasting promotes self control which any Muslim must have.

6   Some Muslims see Ramadan as an annual training programme to recharge the spiritual batteries so that they can carry out their duties to God for the rest of the year.

Eid al'Fit'r

The end of Ramadan is celebrated by a festival on the 1 *Shawwal* (the month after Ramadan). This is the festival of the breaking of the fast and all Muslims should attend the mosque for special prayers to thank God for Ramadan and for the benefits it has brought them. During the prayers the imam will say, 'The religious duties of the first ten days of Ramadan gain the mercy of God, those of the second ten merit his pardon, while those of the last ten save those who do them from the punishment of hell.' These words show that to complete the whole of Ramadan is regarded as a great religious feat which brings with it many blessings. For many Muslims who do not say Salah every day completing Ramadan properly will give them God's forgiveness.

Eid is a very joyful day for Muslims when cards and gifts are exchanged, new clothes are bought for children and families meet up with each other - sometimes in cemeteries so they can remember the dead together. It is a public holiday in Muslim countries.

However, eid must not be confused with festivals in Christianity and other religions. Ramadan is the important religious event not eid.

Eid has very little religious significance. Some scholars believe that Islam is the only religion which does not have any real festivals.

Conclusion on Ramadan

Ramadan is probably the most universally practised of the four practical pillars because it is something everyone does together. It unites the Muslim community and, for those living in a non-Muslim country, gives them a feeling of the power of Islam and how different they are from other religions.

Most Muslims will try to keep at least some of the fast days, though some find the whole month too difficult. This is particularly true for those living in the northern parts of Europe when Ramadan occurs around midsummer e.g. in 1984 Muslims living in the Shetland Isles would have had to fast between the hours of 1.30 a.m. and midnight (eleven hours more fasting than in Mecca). It is almost impossible under such circumstances to carry on a normal life and the coming of industrialisation has caused problems for the observance of Ramadan in some Muslim countries e.g. completing an eight hour shift in the heat of a steel factory without drinking. There is some debate among some Muslim lawyers as to whether the times of Ramadan should be standardised on Mecca, but most Muslims refuse to countenance any changes.

The most important thing about Ramadan is that it reveals and strengthens the unity of Islam and of Muslim families and draws them nearer to God

5. Hajj

'For Hajj are the months well known. If anyone undertakes that duty therein, let there be no obscenity, nor wickdness nor wrangling in the Hajj. And whatever good ye do, be sure God knoweth it.' (Sura 2 v 197) 'Hajj is the Gate of Paradise.' (Hadith)

Hajj is a duty commanded by God and so is the fifth pillar. The regulations in the Qur'an are contained in sura 22 verses 26 - 38, but no chronology or places are given to the rituals.

The regulations for Muslims today are based on a combination of the Qur'an and the Sunna of the Prophet on the pilgrimages he performed in 629, 630 and 631CE.

The conditions Muslims have to fulfil to go on Hajj:

Hajj is the only pillar which Muslims do not have to perform. Muslims can only go on Hajj if:

a) They have sufficient money to leave to care for their dependants whilst they are away from home.

b) They are physically and mentally fit (Hajj is a physically demanding ritual).

Whilst Muslims are on Hajj they must:

1   if a man, wear the *ihram* (pilgrim dress which is two pieces of unsewn cloth one round the waist the other over the shoulder), no head covering is allowed, but you can carry a parasol or umbrella;

2   if a woman, wear a self-coloured garment (usually white) which covers the whole body except face and feet (veils are not worn on Hajj);

3   not cut any hair from their body;

4   refrain from sex, wearing perfumes and wearing rings;

5   not enter into contracts or act as a witness.

What Happens on Hajj ?

1   If pilgrims arrive before the first day of Hajj (7 *Dhu al'hijja*), they should familiarise themselves with the geography of the places on Hajj. However, most pilgrims nowadays arrive on charter flights arriving on the seventh. They have to perform their ablutions before they enter the *haram* of Mecca (the holy area which non-Muslims are forbidden to enter).

2   All the pilgrims on 7 Dhu al'hijja enter the Great Mosque by the *Bab al' Salaam* (Gate of Greeting) and cross the courtyard where they try to kiss the Black Stone at the base of the Ka'ba.

3   They then jog round the Ka'ba seven times (this is called a *tawaf*) and at the end of each circuit they try to touch the Black Stone or the wall of the Ka'ba. Whilst they do this they should be saying special prayers including the Hajj prayer called *talbiya* ('Here I am O my God. Here I am. No partner hast thou, here am I. Truly the praise and the grace are thine and the empire. No partner hast thou, here am I'). The talbiya must be said over and over again during Hajj.

4   Two raka't are performed in the courtyard of the Mosque, then the pilgrims leave via the *Bab al' Safa* and make seven circuits of a covered passageway (called the *Ma'sa*)which now connects the two hills of Safa and Marwa. Some of these circuits are at a walk some at a jog.

5   They then return to the courtyard for midday prayers and a sermon in which the *Sharif* of Mecca outlines the events of Hajj and their significance and gives advice to the pilgrims on how to behave.

6   The next day the pilgrims gather in the Great Mosque and collect sufficient water from the *Zamzam Well* to last them for the Hajj (this is now usually in bottles provided by the Saudi pilgrim guide each group of pilgrims is given). They then walk six miles to Mina for the midday prayers. They stay in Mina in contemplation until Isha prayers after which they walk by night the five miles to Arafat.

7   The next day (9 Dhu al'hijja) is the most important day of the
     pilgrimage and if you miss this, then you must repeat the Hajj. It
     is called *Waquf of Arafat* and all the pilgrims must stand upright on
     the plain in front of the small hill of Arafat and confess their sins
     to God. Between midday and sunset whilst they confess, the chief
     qadi of Mecca preaches a sermon which is broadcast
     simultaneously on Saudi radio so that pilgrims too far away to
     hear, listen on the radio. The pilgrims then jog to Muzdalifa for a
     torchlight *Waquf* followed by another jog to Mina which should be
     reached before daylight.

8   On the way to Mina the pilgrims should have picked up 49 stones
     which they must throw at the three Stoning Pillars shouting
     'Allahu Akbar' with each stone (the talbiya ends after Arafat).
     Then the pilgrims offer their sacrifice to God (usually a lamb, but
     often pilgrims join together to sacrifice a camel). They eat some of
     the meat themselves the rest is to be given to the poor, so (as
     there are so many pilgrims today) the Saudi government puts the
     meat onto refrigerator ships and sends it to poor Muslim
     countries.

     This is the day of eid al'adha and is the only part of Hajj which can
     be joined in by Muslims all over the world.

     Every mosque should have a congregational prayer as on eid
     al'fit'r. Then Muslims should gather as a family and make a
     sacrifice of a sheep or a goat (many Muslims in this country
     sacrifice a chicken). This can be done by a *halal* butcher or by the
     head of household. There should then be a feast with the food and
     the rest should be given to the poor. 'The sacrifice expresses the
     inner feeling of a Muslim that, if need be, he will sacrifice his most
     loved possession for Allah. This is the lesson of the occasion.'
     (Sarwar)

9   For the next two days the pilgrims stone the pillars and on 12 Dhu
     al'hijja are allowed to abandon ihram and the regulations of Hajj.

10   On 13 Dhu al'hijja the pilgrims walk to Mecca and perform a final
     tawaf and circuit of the Ma'sa after which the Hajj is complete.

11   It is traditional to go on to Medina to visit the grave of
     Muhammad and his mosque, but these are carefully arranged so
     that it is impossible to make a circuit because Hajj is worship of
     God not Muhammad.

Reasons For Hajj, other than those in the Qur'an

1   For many Muslims the main reason for going on Hajj is that this
    is what the Prophet did. Everything they do on Hajj is following
    in the footsteps of the Prophet, performing the actions he
    performed in the places he performed them.

2   However, for most Muslims the importance of Hajj is that it
    makes them realise their religion was not something new,
    brought by Muhammad in the seventh century,

>   the pilgrims... behold first the 'plain memorials' of and about
>   the lives of the prophets Ibrahim and Ismail and Allah's affairs
>   with them. They behold secondly the institution of the Hajj
>   itself, living witness to the example and inheritance of Ibrahim
>   and Ismail. (Fateh M. Sandeela)

3   The Ka'ba was built by Adam, destroyed in the Flood, rebuilt by
    Ibrahim at the command of God and made a centre of pilgrimage
    by Ibrahim, it was finally cleansed of idolatry by Muhammad
    who threw out the Meccan idols when he captured Mecca in
    630CE. Making the circuits of the Ka'ba is thus following a long
    tradition. The Black Stone was sent down directly from God to
    Adam to be the main part of the Ka'ba. The Ka'ba is simply a
    cuboid building of undressed granite covered by the black and
    gold cloth of the *kiswan*. The building itself is totally empty
    representing the fact that Islam worships the Lord of all beings
    who cannot be restricted to any particular place.

4   The Ma'sa represents the route travelled by Hagar as she
    searched for water for herself and her young son Ismail (the
    ancestor of the Arabs). The pilgrims run and walk to represent
    her actions. There is also a tradition that Ibrahim was attacked by
    Satan in this valley.

5   The Zamzam Well is the water found by Hagar and Ismail and is
    regarded as holy water because it was made specially for them by
    God.

6   Arafat is the place where Adam and Eve found themselves after
    being thrown out of the Garden of Eden. It was here that Adam
    confessed his sins and was forgiven and was made the first
    prophet of God. The plain of Arafat is also thought to be the plain
    where everyone will be gathered for the Day of Judgement so
    that Muslims confessing their sins at Arafat are prepared for the
    Day of Judgement and might actually make sure that the sins

which they have confessed at Arafat will not count against them when that day comes.

7   The pillars at Mina represent the Devil and remind the pilgrims of the way Satan tried to tempt Ibrahim to disobey God and refuse to sacrifice his son, (there are also stories that the Devil tempted Ismail to disobey his father and that Ismail also stoned the Devil). When pilgrims stone the pillars, they also stone the Devil within themselves and make sure that they will resist evil.The sacrifice at Mina represents the sacrifice which Ibrahim made when he obeyed God and prepared to sacrifice his son and God rewarded him by producing a 'fat ram'. The Qur'an is unclear as to whether this son was Ishaq or Ismail, but nowadays almost all Muslims believe it was Ismail.

The Religious Significance of Hajj

1   The pilgrim has fulfilled the requirements of the fifth pillar as set down in sura 22, therefore he can die happy in this knowledge.

2   The pilgrim has followed the example and actions of the Prophet in the very place that the Prophet himself performed them.

3   The pilgrim has taken part in a very expensive and difficult event to show devotion to God. There are many fatalities every year from crushing, exhaustion or heart attacks. Many Muslims put off Hajj until they retire, because Muslims believe that if they die while performing Hajj, they go straight to heaven without having to wait in the grave for Judgement Day.

4   The pilgrim has taken part in the holiest event in the Muslim calendar and has come as close to God as is possible in this life. The sacred character which is experienced momentarily during Salah is present all the time of Hajj. Everything which is done on Hajj has a symbolic aspect,

> through the circumambulation (tawaf), the pilgrim participates with the angels and other creatures in their circumambulation of the Divine Throne... Arafat is the place for reaching the pinnacle of the consciousness of God... This external act of throwing pebbles at three stone blocks must be accompanied by an inner urge to kill or drive away the satan that is whispering within oneself... Through this sacrifice a pilgrim is symbolically sacrificing himself and fulfilling the obligation of the covenant. (Syed Ali Ashraf)

An Egyptian Muslim, al'Batanuni, said of Hajj,

> If we had not been witness to the raising of the arms and the
> movements of the body during salat and the raising of the
> hands during prayers and the murmurings of the expressions of
> humility, and if we had not heard the beating of the hearts
> before this immeasurable splendour, we would have thought
> ourselves transferred to another life. And truly at that hour we
> were in another world: we were in the House of God and in
> God's immediate presence. (quoted in *Muhammadan Festivals*)

5   The pilgrim becomes aware of the power of God to unite different
races and languages into a common language, a common ritual
and a common brotherhood in Islam.

> Is there in any of the four quarters of the earth a place not quite
> seven square miles in extent where a half a million people
> gather on a pilgrimage, all of whom call on God with one heart
> and one tongue ? And although they differ in race and
> language, they all turn to one Qibla and at the Salat move with
> one motion without any hope other than the grace of the one
> God who has not begotten and is not born and is without equal!
> (Al'Batanuni)

This inter-racial aspect of Hajj has increased rapidly since the
Second World War. There were 60,000 pilgrims on the Hajj of 1939
whereas in 1990 there were over two and a half million pilgrims
from all over the world. New converts, especially those from
Africa south of the Sahara (where Islam is growing rapidly), come
to Mecca to be made aware of the power of Islam and of the unity
of the Muslim brotherhood.

6   The pilgrims can be called *Hajji* when they return home. This is a
title of honour and means they should be highly regarded in the
community. Their sins have been forgiven and so they can now
live a life as a perfect Muslim.

Conclusion on Hajj

For most Muslims Hajj is regarded as the crowning achievement of a
Muslim's life and the unifying element of the Muslim faith.

> The pilgrimage is in a way the biggest of all ibadah. For unless a
> man really loves God he would never undertake such a long
> journey leaving all his near and dear ones behind him. And this

pilgrimage is unlike any other journey. Here his thoughts are concentrated on Allah, his very being vibrates with the atmosphere of intense devotion. When he reaches the holy place, he finds the atmosphere filled with piety and godliness; he visits places which bear witness to the glory of Islam, and all this leaves an indelible impression on his mind which he carries to his last breath... The pilgrimage unites the Muslims of the world into one international fraternity. (Abul Ala Mawdudi)

However, recently some Muslims have begun to challenge this view. They claim that this is what Hajj ought to be, but as it is, it is used by the Saudi authorities to maintain the status quo and make Muslims think that all is well with Islam when, in fact Hajj should be the basis of reform in Islam to make it what it ought to be. These views can be seen clearly in the collection of articles in *Hajj in Focus*.

The Hajj is a great leveller of the distinctions of wealth position and power. But in today's neo-jahiliyya the wealthy and the powerful maintain their distinction even during the Hajj. The mode of transport, the diversity of accommodation based on commercialism, and even the quality of cloth used for ihram, all go to make for the accentuation of these distinctions. This obscenity reaches its peak around the Ka'ba itself when one of the heads of state performs the tawaf. The Ka'ba suffers the indignity of being surrounded by uniformed soldiers carrying arms and wearing boots. An area around the Ka'ba is cleared to allow the rulers of these nation states 'protection', presumably from their own people, in the House of Allah!

The procedure and ritual of the Hajj are so arranged at the present time that the hajji return home none the wiser about the true state of the umma. Nearly two million Muslims gather together in Makkah for the Hajj every year. It is a measure of the success of our ruling classes that this great annual assembly of Muslims poses no threat to the existing order in the Arabian Peninsula or in the world outside. The meaning and manifestation of the Hajj are totally missing from the manner in which two million Muslims perform the ritual year after year. At a time in history when the whole of Palestine, including Jerusalem, is occupied by Israel, the Hajj comes and goes without any effort to transform it into an instrument for the motivation and mobilisation of the Umma to confront its enemies. (*Hajj in Focus*, Kalim Siddiqui)

CHAPTER FOUR

THE SHARI'A
AND THE MUSLIM WAY OF LIFE

The idea that Muhammad was 'the Seal of the Prophets' means that for Islam everything a Muslim needs to know about religion is to be found in the message Muhammad was given (the Qur'an).

The idea that Islam is submission to the will of God; that humans are God's vice-regents put here to make the earth what God wants it to be; that the will of God is revealed in the Qur'an which tells people how to be vice-regents; that there will be a Day of Judgement when people will be judged on how they have behaved as vice-regents; all mean that in Islam there must be a law about how to behave and this law must cover the whole of people's behaviour.

The way in which Islam was established by Muhammad making Medina an umma (religious community) and with Muhammad being both a statesman and a prophet means that from the beginning Islam was concerned with rules and regulations for how to live. Consequently, there was no division in Islam between civil and religious law. There was only one law - the Shari'a.

Shari'a means 'a clear straight path', 'the way in which God wants men to walk'. The whole idea of Shari'a is to set down for Muslims exactly what they should and should not do.

> The Islamic Shari'a removes from human beings harmful burdensome customs and superstitions, aiming to simplify and ease the business of day-to-day living. Its principles are designed to protect man from evil and to benefit him in all aspects of his life. (Yusuf al'Qaradawi)

Where does the Shari'a come from ?

The first source for the Shari'a has to be the Qur'an. This is the word of God and it should contain everything Muslims need to know about how to live their life.

However, as Muslim scholars tried to work out how Muslims should live their lives, they discovered areas not covered by the Qur'an and so they developed **Secondary sources for the Shari'a.**

1   The Sunna (actions, way of life) of the Prophet - if Muhammad was the final prophet, then what he did must be the final example of how a perfect human being should live and his actions will therefore be a part of Shari'a.

2   The Hadith (sayings) of the Prophet - if he was the final prophet what advice he gave to people must be the nearest we can get to God's word. The problem with Hadith is to discover which are genuine ones because, unlike the Qur'an, there are many variations (for details on this refer back to chapter one). Problems arose when Hadith contradicted each other or even contradicted the Qur'an, so other methods had to be arrived at for determining laws.

3   Custom or practice of the Muslim community - this was particularly applied to the Muslim community of Medina because if Muhammad set up the community of Medina, it must follow that their behaviour would be based on his actions

4   Consensus - this is the decisions of the Ulama (a group of Muslim lawyers - *muftis*) who agree that this is the Muslim way to do things. This is very similar to;

5   Opinion - Muslim lawyers who are pious, holy men and have studied the law must be able to give a Muslim opinion on a matter which is not covered by Qur'an, Hadith or Sunna. Opinion refers to one Muslim lawyer, consensus to the opinion of many Muslim lawyers.

6   Analogy - this is the idea that if you cannot find an example in Qur'an, Sunna or Hadith you try to look for an analogy in the Qur'an e.g. if you wanted to know whether snorting coke was lawful for a Muslim, you would look at the Qur'an and see that alcohol is forbidden to Muslims because it intoxicates. Therefore, taking cocaine must be wrong for a Muslim, because it, too, intoxicates.

In the first four centuries of Islam there was much debate as to what the Shari'a was and how it should be defined. The sources above were determined by famous Muslim scholars and gradually their ideas formed into **four Law Schools.**

1   **The Hanifite Law School** (dominant in Turkey, Iraq, the Muslim

states of the former USSR, India and Pakistan). This is the earliest Law School and makes its decisions on the basis of Qur'an, Sunna, Hadith, then analogy and if analogy fails it will use opinion, but not consensus or custom.

2   **The Malikite Law School** (dominant in West Arabia, North Africa, West Africa). This is the second Law School founded by Malik, a native of Medina, which is perhaps why it places custom immediately after Qur'an, Sunna and Hadith. If custom failed, Malik allowed consensus, but only the consensus of the Medinan lawyers. He would not allow analogy or opinion.

3   **The Shafi'ite Law School** (dominant in Egypt, Syria, South Arabia, Indonesia, Malaysia, East Africa). This is the third Law School and bases its principles on Qur'an, Sunna and Hadith, if these fail then he believed consensus was the most important because the combined opinions of Muslim scholars could not be allowed by God to go wrong; only if there was nothing in consensus would Shafi'i allow analogy, but not custom or opinion which was regarded as too individual and divisive.

4   **The Hanbalite Law School** (dominant in Arabia especially as the Wahhabi sect of Saudi-Arabia) This was the final Law School and arose in opposition to the other three because Hanbal thought they had taken things too far and were relying on custom. consensus, analogy or opinion rather than Qur'an, Sunna and Hadith. So he allowed none of them and believed it should be possible to formulate all necessary Muslim laws from Qur'an, Hadith and Sunna.

How does the Shari'a Operate ?

In Muslim countries the law should be determined by the Ulama who should decide which law school their country will follow (this is very difficult where a country has been recently created e.g. Pakistan where traditionally some areas have followed one Law School and some another).

In each town the government must appoint at least one qadi (a mufti who acts as both judge and jury in a case). The way the courts operate is as much religious as legal, since it is assumed that if you swear your innocence on the Qur'an, you must be innocent. The Shari'a which the qadis administer cannot change. Since the finalisation of the Law Schools in about 1100CE, you cannot have any alterations which is why cutting off the hands of thieves etc. (the *Hadd* or canonical punishments) is associated with the Shari'a law.

In the late nineteenth and early twentieth centuries, the impact of the West led many Muslim countries to relegate the Shari'a to the area of family law and use Western legal systems for criminal and other civil laws. Turkey actually abandoned the Shari'a altogether when she adopted the Swiss Civil Code in 1928. However, in the late twentieth century there has been a resurgence of interest in the Shari'a, and a belief among many Muslims that the decline of Islamic civilisation has been due to the rejection of the Shari'a.

As Muslims seek to re-apply the Shari'a, they are also trying to remove the differences between the Law Schools so that there can be no argument as to what the Shari'a is. This is a daunting task as shown by Yusuf al'Qaradawi in his attempt to sort out *The Lawful and the Prohibited in Islam* where in his introduction he states,

> Such a subject, moreover, compels the writer to be definitive concerning many matters about which earlier scholars have differed and contemporary scholars are confused. Consequently to prefer one opinion over another in matters relating to the halal and the haram in Islam requires patience, thoroughness in research and intellectual exertion on the part of the researcher.

On the other hand some Muslim lawyers feel that it is exactly this concept, namely, that there can be no differences between the Shari'a of 630CE and the Shari'a today, which has caused Islam to fail. Subhi Mahmasani suggests,

> the closure of ijtahid (the system of legal enquiry that led to the formation of the four Law Schools) violates the provisions and concepts of Islamic jurisprudence and condemns all Muslims to permanent stagnation and exclusion from the laws of evolution ...The remedy lies in opening what the ancients had closed, or attempted to close. The door of ijtahid should be thrown wide open to anyone juristically qualified.

These two views show the problem of the Shari'a for Islam - although it is supposed to cover every area of life, it has to be adapted for modern living and although it is supposed to be clear and certain, there are inconsistencies and different views.

The Concept of Halal and Haram

A Hadith says, 'The halal is that which Allah has made lawful in His Book, and the haram is that which He has forbidden, and that concerning which He is silent, He has permitted as a favour to you.' From this and various Qur'anic verses, Muslim scholars have agreed that everything Allah has created is halal unless it has been declared haram.

Halal is normally sub-divided into fard (obligatory duties such as the Pillars); *mandub* (recommmended actions performance of which is rewarded but omission of which is not punished such as Du'a prayers); *mubah* (actions permitted by the fact that nothing is said about them so they will neither be rewarded nor punished, such as watching TV).

Haram actions are sometimes subdivided into *makruh* (actions disapproved of but not punished e.g. visiting the graves of saints - some Muslims would include divorce) and haram (forbidden actions which will be punished by law and God).

All Muslim social, moral and economic life is based on these principles and the rest of this chapter is based on them. Although not all Muslims will agree with everything that is stated as Muslim custom, because customs vary from country to country and Law School to Law School, these are the generally accepted Muslim views

The Islamic Attitude to Sex and Marriage

The Qur'an does not say anything specific about sex before marriage, however, there are various statements about avoiding indecency and fornication, 'Come not nigh to shameful deeds whether open or secret', (sura 6 v 151). The verse, 'And among His signs is this that He has created for you mates from among yourselves so that ye may dwell in tranquility with them', (sura 30 v 21) is taken to mean that sex should only occur in marriage.

All Muslims now believe that sex must be restricted to marriage and this has certain connotations for Muslim social life. *Zina* (sex outside marriage) is haram and as Yusuf al'Qaradawi says,

> When Islam prohibits something, it closes all the avenues of approach to it. This is achieved by prohibiting every step and

every means leading to haram. Accordingly, whatever excites passions, opens ways for illicit sexual relations between a man and a woman and promotes indecency and obscenity is haram.

This is why the sexes are kept separate as much as possible and why women and men must wear modest baggy clothes which do not draw attention to their sexual characteristics. Men are forbidden to wear silk or gold and women must have everything but face, hands and feet (*hijab* dress) covered when in public. These rules are also based on Qur'anic statements such as sura 33 v 33 - 39.

Celibacy is regarded as makruh if not actually haram. After all the Prophet married several times and a good Sunni Muslim must follow the example of the Prophet and so he should marry.

'As long as he possesses the means to marry, the Muslim is not permitted to refrain from marriage on the grounds that he has dedicated himself to the service or the worship of Allah.' (Yusuf al'Qaradawi)

Marriage Form

Marriage is a gift from God, 'He is the One who has created you all from a single person and made its mate of like nature in order that he might dwell with her in love', (sura 7 v 189). However, the marriage itself is seen as a contract rather than a sacrament. There is no concept in Islam of the marriage being an exchange of eternal vows made before God.

For a marriage to be valid, a relation or representative of the bride must ask the bride in front of two witnesses if she agrees to the marriage proposal of the bridegroom (this will contain a statement on the *mahr* - the amount of money which the groom will put in trust for the bride and which becomes hers if he divorces her or if he dies), then the relative or representative goes to the bridegroom who is with the *mullah* or imam and the imam will ask the representative if the bride has agreed to the marriage. Then he will ask the groom if he is still offering to marry the bride. If he agrees, then the marriage contract is signed and the marriage is complete.

Most Muslim weddings involve not only the signing of the contracts, but also special prayers and Qur'anic readings by an imam. All Muslim weddings are followed by some form of feast or celebration, and it is essential that the wedding should be witnessed by the community.

The restrictions on contact between the sexes after puberty are the reason for the popularity of arranged marriages. However, although a marriage may be arranged, it is still permissible for the bride and groom to meet each other before they agree to a marriage, 'It is permissible for a Muslim man to see the woman to whom he intends to propose marriage before taking further steps, so that he can enter into the marriage knowing what is ahead of him.' (Yusuf al'Qaradawi)

Many Muslims in the UK now advertise for marriage partners in Asian magazines and newspapers.

Restrictions on who a Muslim can marry

The Qur'an says that Muslim men can marry Jews or Christians as well as Muslims, but Muslim women can only marry Muslim men sura 4 v 22 - 25.

Men are also allowed to marry more than one wife up to a maximum of four but with certain restrictions, 'Then marry such women as seem good to you, two, three or four at a time. If you fear that you will not act justly, then marry one woman only... that is more likely to keep you from committing an injustice.' (sura 4 v 3)

Islam has the same restrictions on marrying blood relatives that are common to all societies.

The Status of Women

There is no doubt that Islam raised the status of women from what it had been in Arabia. However, the Qur'anic verse 'Women have the same rights in relation to their husbands as are expected in all decency of them; while men stand a step above them' (sura 2 v 228) and 'Men are the ones who support women since God has given some persons advantages over others', (sura 4 v 34) mean that men and women can never be fully equal in Islam.

The Qur'an gives women the right to own property. They also have the right to inherit, earn money and be educated. Indeed several Muslim lawyers have argued that women have the right to become imams and mullahs.

> Generally speaking, in the Muslim world of the early medieval times, there was not any bar or prohibition on women pursuing studies - on the contrary, the religion encouraged it. As a result of

this many women became famous as religious scholars, writers, poets, doctors and teachers in their own rights such as Nafisa a descendant of Ali who was such a great authority on hadith that Imam al'Shafi'i sat in her circle at Fustat. (Aisha Lemu)

Nevertheless, the different status is shown by the Qur'anic regulations that women can only inherit half of what a man inherits and that a woman's testimony in court only counts for half of a man's.

All of this, for Muslims, simply reflects the differences between men and women which result from God's creation of two sexes. The biological function of woman is to bear children and the biological function of man is to provide for the woman and her children which is why he needs to inherit more.

An average man is stronger, heavier, harder in muscles and taller than an average woman. Women can become pregnant and bear children, but men cannot. Women tend to be sensitive, emotional and tender while men are comparatively less emotional and more practical. Throughout history men and women have never been treated the same. Islam has given women the right position and has not attempted to violate divine laws. (Ghulam Sarwar)

Nevertheless, the teaching of Islam is that women should have total equality in religion and education. The Qur'an states, 'Whoever works righteousness, man or woman, and has faith, verily to him will We give a new life.' (sura 16 v 97) A Hadith states, 'The search for knowledge is a duty for every Muslim, male or female.'

Family Life

The function of the family is to provide care and promote the acceptance of Islam by the children. The role of the woman is most important in the family. She is the one who should keep a halal home making sure that all the food and dress laws are kept and that the children learn to say their prayers properly and go to mosque school.

The role of the husband is to provide financially for the family as best he can according to his means. It is also his duty to introduce his child to Islam by whispering the Shahada in the baby's ear as soon after birth as possible; to organise the aqiqa ceremony, if this is done, (aqiqa is the naming ceremony, when the baby's first hair is cut and a gift given to the poor); to ensure a good marriage for his children.

Children are a gift from God and the way Muslims treat their children is part of God's test, 'Your riches and your children may be but a trial...' (sura 64 v 15).

If you are not given the gift of children, then this must be God's will and adoption is not permitted, 'Nor has He made your adopted sons your sons,' (sura 33 v 4).

> The type of adoption which has been abolished by Islam is that kind which makes a boy a member of the family with all the rights of inheritance, the permissibility of mixing freely with other members of the household, the prohibition of marriage and so on. But the word adoption is also used in another sense in Islam - that is when a man brings home an orphan or a foundling to rear, to educate and to treat as his own... However, he does not attribute the child to himself, nor does he give him the rights which the Shari'a reserves for natural children. (Yusuf al'Qaradawi)

Islam is very concerned with patrial lineage because the Qur'an states that it is divinely ordained. This is why some Muslims would justify polygamy so that if a wife is barren, then she and the new wife can share the joy of children.

Muslim parents are commanded to look after their children, but children are also commanded to care for their parents,

> We have enjoined on man kindness to his parents: in pain did his mother bear him, and in pain did she give him birth. The carrying of the child to its weaning is thirty months. At length, when he reaches the age of full strength and attains forty years, he says, 'O my Lord! Grant me that I may be grateful for Thy favour which Thou hast bestowed upon me and upon both my parents, and that I may work righteousness such as thou mayest approve...' (sura 46 v 15)

From this comes the concept of the extended family of at least three generations living together. This is also hinted at in the many Qur'anic verses which say that you should look after your poor relatives and the orphans.

The importance of the extended family in Islam can be seen from the laws governing inheritance. The Qur'an states that a maximum of one third of an estate can be left to who you want, the other two thirds must be left in the following sequence: spouse, parents, brothers, sisters, children. The rules are extremely complex and their implementation by the Law Schools has led to situations where, because someone's parents are still alive, children receive nothing. However, this is the whole point of the extended family - those children will be looked after.

As Kurshid Ahmad said in reply to a question from a Muslim who only had daughters and objected to his brothers and sisters inheriting from him when they would not have if he had had sons,

> The Islamic system does take care of even such exceptional situations. Girls in the situation you describe would not be thrown to the dogs, they would be protected in the family, and the family does not mean just father and mother. The family represents a much extended relationship. Your brothers, your sisters, your parents, all of them are part of the family and in the absence of any one of the members, they will be looking after the affairs of your children. (Report of a discussion printed in *Women in Islam*)

The family should be the basis of economic and social life which is why some Muslims object to Welfare States because they take away family duties.

Divorce

Although Islam places much emphasis on family life, divorce is allowed and is very easy to obtain. The Qur'an gives no regulations on the grounds for divorce, but states that a woman must receive her mahr if her husband divorces her; there must be a waiting period to see if she is pregnant; that if she is pregnant she cannot then be divorced until the child is two years old; that re-marriage of divorcees is expected, but if she does not re-marry, the husband must provide for his wife for at least two years (sura 2 v 228-232).

The Law Schools have determined two types of divorce *talaq* (when only one party wants a divorce) and *kuhl* (where there is an agreed divorce). Men can have either type and in a talaq divorce simply say 'I divorce you' three times in front of witnesses. Women can only have a kuhl divorce (and they lose their mahr) or a talaq divorce if they can prove their husband is impotent, insane or suffering from venereal disease, in which cases she keeps the mahr.

Divorce causes problems of custody of children in Islam. The basic teaching is that the mother should have custody until the child reaches puberty. However, the fact that in Islam your religion comes from the father means that fathers can apply for custody if they can prove that the mother is not a good Muslim. Also if the wife re-marries, then the child goes back into the father's custody unless she re-marries a close relative of her former husband.

> In all the schools of Islam, the mother of the child has responsibility for care and control of the child for the first few years of the child's life. The father, who has rights over the child as wali (guardian), retains the overall rights and indeed the powers of guardianship, (*A Textbook on Muslim Personal Law* David Pearl).

Although divorce is so easy in Islam, it is frowned upon. According to Abu Douad, the Prophet Muhammad said, 'Among lawful things, divorce is most hated by Allah.' Furthermore the fact that most marriages are arranged by families means that there are terrific social pressures for a marriage to succeed and this reduces the need for divorce.

Contraception, Abortion and Genetic Engineering

Some Muslims believe that the Qur'an bans contraception , 'Kill not your children on a plea of want.' (sura 6 v 151)

However, Yusuf al'Qaradawi and Shaykh Abdullah al'Qalqili (Grand Mufti of Jordan) both claim that contraception is halal for Muslims because there are several Hadith which refer to Companions of the Prophet practising *coitus interruptus* (the earliest form of contraception banned by Judaism) and the Prophet agreed to it. Therefore, if that form of contraception is allowed to Muslims, the rest must be as well. However, for Muslims contraception must only be used to limit the size of a family - it is a Muslim's duty to have children.

There is much more controversy in Islam concerning abortion. Those Muslims who ban contraception would use the same Qur'anic verse to ban abortion. They would say that God creates life and He will provide for any children that are produced.

Yusuf al'Qaradawi agrees to a large extent with this view, 'While Islam permits preventing pregnancy for valid reasons, it does not allow doing violence to the pregnancy once it occurs.' However, he claims that Islam allows abortion if the mother's life is in danger, 'If, say the jurists, after the baby is completely formed, it is reliably established that the continuation of the pregnancy would necessarily result in the death of the mother, then, in accordance with the general principle of the Shari'a, that of choosing the lesser of two evils, abortion must be performed.'

Shaykh Abdullah al'Qalqili takes a much more liberal view,

> The jurists give examples to illustrate the meaning of the excuse for abortion as in ibn Abidin who says, 'like the mother who has a baby still unweaned and who becomes pregnant and her milk ceases and the father is unable to hire a wet nurse to save the life of his baby.' The jurists also state that it is permissible to take medicine for abortion so long as the embryo is still unformed in the human shape. The period of the unformed shape is given as a hundred and twenty days. The jurists think that during this state the embryo is not yet a human being. A report says that Umar (the second caliph) does not regard abortion as infanticide when the foetus is already past the limit.

This *fatwa* by a mufti can be used by Muslims in the West to accept the abortion laws of countries like the UK. However, there is much disagreement among Muslims on the issue of abortion.

Little has been written about the Muslim attitude to genetic engineering, although, if a Muslim followed the fatwa of Qalqili on abortion, there would be no reason to reject such things as *in vitro fertilisation* even though some embryos are likely to be killed.

Yusuf al'Qaradawi does state that artificial insemination by the father is permissible in Islam, but artificial insemination by a donor is not. He bases this on a fatwa by Shaykh Shultat,

> There is no doubt that insemination by a donor other than the husband is a more serious crime and detestable offence than adoption, for the child born of such insemination incorporates in itself the result of adoption - the introduction of an alien element into the lineage - in conjunction with the offence of adultery... By this action the human being is degraded to the level of an animal.

Regulations on other Aspects of Social Life

Islam has several **food regulations**. Muslims are not allowed to eat carrion, pork, animals devoured by wild beasts, animals strangled to death, the blood of any animal, carnivorous animals, animals killed without invoking the name of God (see sura 2 v 172).

Meat Muslims are allowed to eat is called halal and is meat which has been slaughtered by the neck vein being slit and the blood drained whilst the name of Allah is invoked. Plus all fish, vegetables etc. as long as no animal fat (which is haram) has been used.

So a Muslim can only eat vegetarian cheese (because normal cheese is made with a small amount of animal rennet) and any crisps, biscuits etc. which are made with vegetable oils rather than animal fats. They can eat any *kosher* food because any food which is permitted for Jews is permitted for Muslims because Jews slaughter in the same way and Jewish food laws are even stricter than Muslim ones.

Sura 5 v 93-4, 'O ye who believe! Intoxicants and gambling, and divination by arrows are an abomination... eschew such abomination that ye may prosper', is the basis for the Muslim prohibition of alcohol. Not only is a Muslim not allowed to drink alcohol, but there are many Hadith stating that a Muslim must not have alcohol in his house, sell alcohol, give alcohol as a gift or even sell produce such as grapes or hops to someone who is going to make alcohol from them, 'It is reported that a man brought a cask of wine to the Prophet as a gift. The Prophet informed him that Allah had prohibited it. "Shall I not sell it?" asked the man. "The One who prohibited drinking it, has also prohibited that it be given as a gift to the Jew," said the Prophet. "Then what shall I do with it?" asked the man. "Pour it on the ground," the Prophet replied.'

The Arabic word *khamr* used in the Qur'an is translated as intoxicant rather than alcohol. Therefore, 'drugs such as marijuana, cocaine, opium and the like are definitely included in the prohibited category of khamr.' (Yusuf al'Qaradawi)

The same Qur'anic verse bans gambling. 'While permitting a variety of games and sports, Islam prohibits any game which involves betting, that is which has an element of gambling in it... What is known as the lottery or raffle is also a form of gambling.' (Yusuf al'Qaradawi)

These regulations do not apply in extreme cases e.g. if you are prescribed medicine with alcohol that is all right; if you are shipwrecked and the only thing between you and starving to death is bacon, then you can eat it. Islam is a practical religion and teaches the dignity of work, 'It is better that a man should take a rope and bring a bundle of wood on his back to sell so that Allah may preserve his honour than that he should beg from people.' (Hadith quoted by Bukhari and Muslim)

However, a Muslim must only work in trades that do not involve anything that is haram, and that would not just mean those which involve lending money at interest, alcohol, gambling, sex, pork, making statues, but also cheating, injustice and making exorbitant profits.

The Shari'a covers every aspect of social life. Qaradawi deals with all sorts of topics in *The Lawful and Prohibited in Islam* from whether a Muslim can have a tattoo, to what films to see at the cinema.

Economic Life

The Qur'an forbids the lending of money at interest (*riba*, usury), 'They say,"trade is like usury" but God hath permitted trade and forbidden usury', (sura 2 v 275). There are many Qur'anic quotations to show that those who live off interest will go to hell. Therefore, a Muslim society should be organised without interest. Muslim banks should share their profits rather than charge and give interest e.g. they lend money to a business and when the business begins to make money then it gives a certain percentage of its profits to the bank which shares that with the investors. Instead of building societies Muslims should pool their savings and lend it all to one family to buy a house, and as soon as they have paid it off, lend it to another family.

Muslims believe that banning interest will share out wealth because interest takes money from the poor and gives it to the rich whereas Islam takes money from the rich and gives it to the poor.

Both fundamentalists and modernisers believe what is wrong with most Muslim countries is that they do not have a proper Muslim economic system. Muslim economists claim that Islam is quite different from both socialism and capitalism. Unlike socialism it believes in free enterprise and market forces; unlike capitalism it bans lending at interest and aims to spread wealth more fairly.

Conflicting Attitudes

There are two types of Muslim today who want Islam to change from traditionalism.

Modernisers think that Islam has lost its roots and that it needs reforming so that it reflects the true religion of God. They tend to have western education and usually reject Sunna, Hadith and Law Schools in favour of the Qur'an and strict reasoning from it.

Fundamentalists agree that Islam has lost its roots, but feel that Islam needs to go back to Sunna and Hadith and take them more seriously e.g. they would attack Muslim fathers who marry off their daughters without their consent, but would accept polygamy, arranged marriages etc.

The modernisers feel that Muslim attitudes to women and marriage need much reform. They accept the extended family but claim the equality of men and women; the need for equal divorce rights; the ending of polygamy etc. They base these claims solely on the Qur'an. For example, they claim that polygamy should be banned because the Qur'an says, 'If you fear you will not act justly, then marry one woman only.' No man can act justly to more than one woman at a time except the Prophet himself, therefore, polygamy was only intended for prophets.

An extreme example of the modernising view can be seen in this statement by Asaf Fyzee, former vice-chancellor of Kashmir University,

> It must be realised that religious practices have become soulless ritual; that large numbers of decent Muslims have ceased to find solace or consolation in the traditional forms of prayer and fasting; that good books on religion are not being written for modern times; that women are treated badly, economically and morally; and that political rights are denied to them even in fairly advanced countries... that the beneficial laws of early Islam have in many instances fallen behind the times and that the futile attempt to plant an Islamic theocracy in any modern state or fashion life after the pattern of early Islam is doomed to failure... Islam must be re-interpreted or else its traditional form may be lost beyond retrieve.

It must be remembered, however, that modernisers are a very small group within Islam. Much more numerous and influential are the fundamentalists.

The fundamentalists take on the West and defend the traditional Muslim teachings on women and the family in many ways. They claim that Muslim marriages are far more successful because of lower divorce rates than the West; that polygamy is better for women than men taking mistresses; that the differences between men and women are an essential part of life and that the decline of the West is connected with the rise of feminism. This is why wherever fundamentalism is successful, the first thing that happens is that women are forced to adopt the hijab dress.

> Islam is a religion of common sense and in line with human nature. It recognises the realities of life... Allah has not made man and woman identical and so it would be against nature to try to have total equality between a man and a woman. That would destroy the social balance. Society would not prosper, but would instead have insoluble problems such as broken marriages, illegitimate children and the break-up of family life. These problems are already rife in Western society. Schoolgirl pregnancies, an increase in abortion, divorce and many other problems have cropped up because of a permissive outlook and the so-called freedom of women. (Ghulam Sarwar)

The Concept of Jihad

This is one of the most misunderstood beliefs of Islam in the western world. Jihad means to struggle or strive and in Islam there is a Greater and a Lesser Jihad. Though it is true that some Muslims dispute which is which, the generally accepted views of Muslims in this country are what we will discuss here.

1. The Greater Jihad

The aim of a Muslim is to live the perfect Muslim life and this, whether you live in a Muslim or a non-Muslim society, is a definite struggle. As Sarwar says, 'a Muslim learns to control his own bad desires and actions.'

So in the Greater Jihad there is the struggle of each individual Muslim to perform the Five Pillars properly and follow the Shari'a of Islam exactly. This is what Muhammad did which is why Muslims follow his Sunna.

The whole life of a Muslim should therefore be a struggle to be 'pleasing to Allah', so that when the Last Day comes they will receive Allah's favour and enter paradise.

Jihad is concerned with establishing right (*maruf*) and removing evil (*munkar*) from yourself. It is Jihad which stops a Muslim from being a hypocrite - as the Qur'an says, 'Why say ye that which ye do not? Grievously odious is it in the sight of God that ye say that which ye do not.' (sura 61 v 2)

By the effort of the Greater Jihad Muslims make sure that they practice Islam and do not merely talk about how good Islam is. Once a Muslim has done this he/she can begin their struggle to remove the haram from society and thereby make the world the place God wants it to be.

2. The Lesser Jihad

This is to struggle to remove evil from society. Therefore, it is the struggle of the Muslim community rather than the Muslim individual. Some Muslim thinkers have said that underdevelopment, unfair trading, the gap between rich and poor, reliance on interest etc. are major evils which require a Muslim Jihad to remove them from society (especially from Muslim societies). This is why some Muslim thinkers in Muslim countries think that the Lesser Jihad should be directed to reforms in their own countries rather than calling for jihads against other countries.

It is true that the concept of Jihad requires that once perfect Islam has been established in the individual and then in the Muslim community, it is the duty of the Muslim to struggle to make the whole world 'the abode of peace'. For without Islam the world will always be at war. However, the struggle to convert the world must be a peaceful one. A war Jihad (what we know in the West as 'Holy War') can only be fought in self-defence, 'Fight in the cause of God those who fight you, but do not transgress the limits; for God loveth not the transgressors.' (sura 2 v 190)

Consequently, the orthodox Muslim teaching today is that a holy war can only be called against an aggressor which threatens Islam. This was why the Afghan rebels called themselves *mujaheedin* because they were struggling against a communist government which was replacing the Shari'a with non-Muslim state laws.

A Jihad could be called against Salman Rushdie because he had attacked Islam, though there is much argument amongst Muslim lawyers on this as they do not feel a Jihad can be called against an individual.

Much of the feeling about Jihad as 'holy war' arises from the way in which Islam originated in Medina and Mecca. It originated as a result of wars and spread through the Middle East as a result of wars. Some Muslims feel that they should fight for the faith, particularly as the Qur'an says that those who die on Jihad will go straight to heaven without waiting for the Day of Judgement, 'Think not of those who are slain in God's way as dead. Nay they live finding their sustenance in the presence of their Lord.' (sura 3 v 169)

However, the regulations of the Law Schools make it difficult for a holy war ever to be called because it must be led by a religious leader chosen by the whole community and renowned for his piety and religion; there must be a prospect of success; the enemies must first be invited to accept Islam peacefully; all the soldiers must be faithful Muslims well-versed in the teachings of Islam.

For Muslims in this country, Jihad is a personal and social struggle, not a war, 'Jihad is the use of all our energies and resources to establish the Islamic system of life, in order to gain Allah's favour.' (Ghulam Sarwar)

CHAPTER FIVE

THE LIFE OF THE PROPHET

What follows is based on the evidence for Muhammad's life as found in the early biographies of ibn Ishaq, ibn Hisham and al'Waqidi. These are the basis of almost all the current biographies by both Muslim and Western scholars

The Background to the Life of Muhammad

Muslim scholars often refer to the period in Arabia before the Call of Muhammad as *Jahiliyya* - (days of ignorance). For some this means they were days when the people of Arabia were uneducated and uncivilised,

> In that benighted era, there was a territory where darkness lay even heavier than elsewhere... Arabia stood isolated, cut off by vast tracts of desert... There was no law except the law of the strongest... Whatever notions they had of morals, culture and civilisation were primitive in the extreme... They worshipped stones, trees, idols, stars and spirits; in short everything conceivable except God... They revelled in adultery, gambling and drinking. (Abul Ala Mawdudi).

For others they mean the days when the Arabs were ignorant of the truth of Islam despite the work of the prophets Ibrahim and Ismail in Arabia,

> Gradually the entire region suffered a terrible deprivation of the monotheistic tradition and sank into the Age of Ignorance. People forgot God and succumbed to the temptations of the world and the lower self. (Jafar Qasimi)

1. The Social Background

Arabia had never been a great empire or civilisation, though people from Arabia had frequently migrated to the empires of the Fertile

Crescent surrounding Arabia which had been the birthplace of civilisation.

Arabia was a desert with a scattering of oases which provided water and vegetation for life. The only fertile part of Arabia was a small strip of land in the South bordering the Indian Ocean.

The Arabs were tribal (groups of people with a common ancestor) and divided. The main economy of the area was trade between the South and the North. The trade winds brought sailing ships from India to Aden in the South. Every year a caravan of merchants would be sent from Mecca with goods brought from either the Byzantine Empire to the North or the Sassanian Empire to the West. These were traded for the Indian produce which was then taken to the North or West to be sold. Mecca was approximately the half-way point between Aden and Syria and so occupied an important position on the trade route.

This trade had been dominated by South Arabia, but in the early sixth century their King had converted to Judaism and his Christian subjects appealed to Abyssinia for help. The Abyssinians invaded the South, but the conflict weakened both powers so that in 580CE the Sassanian Empire was able to take over the South of Arabia.

This conflict allowed a power vacuum to develop in Arabia of which Mecca took advantage. Muhammad's great grandfather, Hashim, increased the Meccan role in the yearly trade cycle. He obtained charters from the Byzantines, the Sassanians and the Abyssinians for Arab traders to move freely in these areas. Then he established a trading system in central Arabia so that traders could move freely. It was an alliance of Arab (Bedouin) tribes around Mecca to promote free trade. It was called al'hums and was based on the religion of the Ka'ba. These tribes called themselves the people of Allah and agreed not to fight each other in return for a share in the profits of the trade caravans.

This had increased the wealth of the area, but this wealth was not being evenly divided. Certain clans of the tribe of Quraysh in Mecca (mainly the Makhzum and Umayyad clans) were making vast sums of money, whilst others (such as Muhammad's own clan the Hashemites) were becoming poorer. The social system was based on clans, and there was no machinery for dealing with discontent.

Each clan had a council of elders (the heads of the extended families within the clan) who elected one of their members as a shaykh. He could rule on disputes on the basis of Sunna (the way in which the ancestors had done things), but there was no way of dealing with any new social or economic situations. The only method of determining disputes betwen clans was vendetta (you kill one of my clan and we'll kill one of yours) or war. Women were of a low social status, and female children were often killed at birth.

Other parts of Arabia were much more socially advanced than Mecca (e.g. Yathrib - Medina), perhaps because of the presence of Christians and Jews, of whom there were very few in Mecca.

Social and economic changes were taking place in Mecca and the system was finding it difficult to cope with them.

2. The Political Background

Perhaps Western Muslim authors think that life before Muhammad was so backward because they have inherited the Western view that if Europe was backward, so was the whole world. This was very untrue with regard to 600 CE. Whilst Western Europe was in the Dark Ages, the Roman Empire had survived in the East where it was known as the Byzantine Empire. It was an imposingly advanced and civilised society.

In the East was the great Sassanian Empire ruling from China to Iraq and from North India to the Caspian Sea. It had an advanced agricultural system based on irrigation and its own philosophies, literature etc.

Both these empires had a long history of civilisation and had a type and standard of living not reached in Western Europe until the middle of the nineteenth century.

However, these two great powers were at war with each other from 614 - 628CE and religious disputes were occurring in the areas on the edge of Arabia.

3. The Religious Background

It is difficult to generalise about the whole of Arabia as there were so many religious differences. However, if we take the area of the Hijaz (the area of North West Arabia covering Mecca and Medina) we can make certain points:

1   **Bedouin polytheism** - This was the religion of the majority of the population - those Arabs who were still nomads, or those

who had settled in oases fairly recently.

Like most nomads, they were rather **animistic** (they thought of strange objects - rocks, trees, springs etc. - as being inhabited by spirits). They believed in *jinn* - the spirits of the desert who could be good or evil and who were likely to approach lone travellers in the desert. They also believed in pilgrimage to the spots inhabited by the spirits where believers tried to touch the object so some of the holiness would rub off on them.

Bedouin polytheism was centred on Mecca where the Ka'ba was the main centre of pilgrimage. They believed in many gods including al'Manat (the goddess of fate), al'Uzza (the all-powerful goddess of love) - who were daughters of Allah (the chief God) and his wife Allat. There were many other gods and goddesses whose names have not been preserved. Apparently there were at least 300 statues of gods and goddesses in the Ka'ba when Muhammad captured it in 630CE.

It is probable that this polytheism was based on the more advanced polytheism of the ancient southern empire of Arabia. Certainly the Bedouin believed that the gods lived in the sky and they believed Allah was immaterial. There was very little mythology about the gods, no holy literature and very little organised worship other than the pilgrimage. However, all meat had to be slaughtered before idols as a type of sacrifice. As there were no holy books, there was no moral code. As long as you made the odd prayer and went on pilgrimage and made the sacrifice everything would be all right.

Meccan polytheism was based on trade and had little real religious content, 'from the very beginning religion was inseparable from trade', (M.A.Shaban).

2   **Judaism** - This had arrived in Arabia as far back as 590BCE when Jews had fled Israel after its capture by the Babylonians. There had been a large migration of Jews in the second century CE, when the Romans banned Jews from living in Palestine and the Jews tried to escape from the Roman Empire. There were several Jewish clans in the Hijaz and they had converted many Arabs to Judaism. It was often difficult to differentiate between Jews and Arab converts to Judaism. There were very few Jews in Mecca, but it would have been impossible for Meccan traders not to be aware of Jews and their beliefs.

It is possible that Medina had been a Jewish city and leader of a Jewish trade network, 'in the light of the close connections between the Madinan Jews and other Jewish communities in Arabia, it is not unreasonable to suggest that a Jewish trade network existed there at the time,' (M.A.Shaban).

The Jews had been successful in making converts, but there was a difficulty in accepting non-Jews as full members of 'the People of God'.

3   **Christianity** - This was the main religion in South, North and East Arabia. It had been the state religion of South Arabia where there was a Christian cathedral at Sana. In the desert itself there were Christian monks and hermits who were often visited by the trading caravans. In Mecca there were a few Christians and Muhammad's wife, Khadijah, had a Christian cousin, Waraqa.

However, there were some major problems over Christianity's belief about Jesus being the Son of God. Most Christians believed that this meant he was God - the doctrine of the Trinity (that although God is one he reveals himself in three ways as Father, Son and Holy Spirit). This was hard for uneducated people to differentiate from a belief in three gods. If Jesus was the Son of God, did that mean he was a man when he was on earth, or God, or a mixture of the two? If he was a man, how could he be the second person of the Trinity? If he was God, how could he pray to himself?

These problems had led to varieties within Christian belief and these different groups were often involved in violent conflict with each other:

The Orthodox believed in the Trinity and in Jesus being both God and Man at the same time - a divine mystery which humans cannot understand. This is what the creeds say and was the dominant belief in the Byzantine Empire and in Western Europe.

The Nestorians based their belief on Luke 3 v 22 'Thou art my beloved Son, today I have begotten thee.' They believed Jesus was only a man who became Son of God through what he did on earth and only became divine after the resurrection. The Arab tribes of the Hira (the East of Arabia) and the Sassanian Empire were Nestorian.

The Monophysites believed that Jesus was simply God and that he only appeared to become man, really he was God all the time. They were mainly to be found in Egypt, Syria and the tribes of South and North Arabia.

Most Muslim authors claim that Judaism and Christianity in Arabia were in a corrupted state 'The religions of the Jews and Christians at that time were so corrupted that they no longer had any appeal to reason and wisdom,' (Ghulam Sarwar).

4   **Hanifs** - There were a few Arab thinkers who had given up on Bedouin polytheism and accepted the idea of one God, but who could not accept either Judaism or Christianity. They often spent a lot of time in the desert praying and were looking for a more Arab form of monotheism. They refused to eat meat offered to idols. There was one such *hanif* in Mecca who Muhammad knew, Zayd ibn Am'r.

Conclusion on the Background

Clearly, Arabia, especially the area around Mecca, was in a social and religious situation ready for change, ready for a new religion of the Arabs.

Muslim authors see this as God preparing the situation for the emergence of Islam,

If we cast a glance at the world atlas, we find that no other country could have been more suitable than Arabia for the much needed world religion. It is situated right in the middle of Asia and Africa and Europe is not far away... Look at the history of the era too, and you will find that no other people were more suited to be endowed with this Prophet than the Arabs... It was, therefore, a manifestation of God's great wisdom that He chose Arabia as the birth-place of the World Prophet, (Abul Ala Mawdudi).

Muhammad's Early Life

There are many stories concerning the birth of Muhammad which try to show how special he was before his birth. Even the year of his birth (traditionally 570 CE) was regarded as a prestigious one. It was the year when the Abyssinians attacked Mecca with elephants in revenge for Meccan attacks on Christianity and the takeover of Yemenite trade. Muhammad's grandfather, Abd' al Muttalib, was the protector of the

Ka'ba and defeated the Abyssinian army (which was regarded as a miracle).

Muhammad was therefore born into a prestigious clan (Hashemite) of the ruling tribe of Mecca, the Quraysh. His grandmother had connections with the ruling tribe of Yathrib (Medina) and through her and his great grandfather Hashim, Muhammad had connections throughout Arabia.

However, although Muhammad's background appears privileged, his life was far from privileged. His father, Abd'Allah, died before Muhammad was born. He spent his first two years in the care of his foster mother, Halima, and then when he was six, his mother, Amina, died. He was put into the care of his grandfather, but he died two years later and Muhammad was left to the care of his uncle, abu Talib, who was now the leader of the Hashemite clan.

Many Muslims think this is what the Qur'anic verse 'Did we not find thee an orphan and shelter thee?' (sura 93) refers to.

During his childhood his clan declined greatly in importance mainly because abu Talib wanted to protect the old trade network of al'Hums set up by Hashim and this relied on sharing profits rather than making the most you could for yourself. Other clans stepped in and made profits for themselves (mainly the Umayyad and Makhzum clans) by reneging on their contract with the Yemen. Muhammad was employed in the trading business (though some traditions say he spent his early youth as a shepherd).

The biographies record a story of Muhammad being in a caravan train with his uncle which stopped at a monastery. The adults went in for a meal and Muhammad was left outside to look after the camels. One of the monks said he had had a vision of a prophet with the party and he asked if he could look for the mark of the prophet on the Meccans. However, he could not find it, so he asked if all the party had been seen and when he found that Muhammad was outside, he went to inspect him and discovered the mark of the prophet between his shoulder blades.

How Muhammad was Prepared for Prophethood

There are many similar stories which reveal how the people of Mecca came to see Muhammad as a wise and just man. He was the only man who could manage to find a way of replacing the Black Stone when the Ka'ba was repaired, without any clans losing face. He was present at the inaugural meeting of the League of the Virtuous in which the smaller clans gathered together to protect the honesty of Meccan trade against the wealthy clans who were threatening to dishonour their debts to the Yemen so that they could corner the trade for themselves. He was also involved in 'the Wicked Wars' in which the Meccans defeated the Central Arabian tribes of Hawazin, thus confirming their dominance of the Arabian trade routes.

Muhammad obviously learnt the techniques of trading, diplomacy and warfare during these years and by the time he was 21, he was sufficiently renowned to be employed as trading manager by a wealthy widow, Khadijah. Some Western biographers have concluded from this that Muhammad must have been literate, but the biographies assert that he never learnt to read or write.

Muslim scholars believe that even at this stage Muhammad had a unique reputation in Mecca, 'Even before his prophethood, Muhammad (pbuh) was the judge and referee of the Quraysh at the time of their disputes and crises. He earned the names of al'Amin (the trustworthy) and as' Sadiq (the truthful),' (Ghulam Sarwar).

Muhammad and Khadijah got along so well that by 595CE he married her. According to Muslim tradition she was 15 years older than him, but that would make her 40 when they married and as she bore him at least six children, this seems very unlikely. They certainly seem to have had a good marriage and even though the two sons she bore him died in infancy, Muhammad did not practise polygamy until after her death. It was the daughters of Muhammad and Khadijah who gave Muhammad his grandchildren.

Between 595 and 610CE Muhammad became more and more interested in religion. According to the earliest biography, it was during this time that Muhammad met a hanif, Zayd ibn Am'r, who greatly impressed him. His own household also had two Christians - a young slave, Zayd ibn Harith, and his wife's cousin, Waraqa.

Muhammad, therefore, had contact with monotheists and was finding Meccan polytheism more and more offensive. The frequent wars, the greed and dishonesty of the leaders of Meccan polytheism were particularly upsetting him.

So Muhammad had experience of managing affairs, solving problems, dealing with crises and had been involved in war before his deep involvement in religion.

Muhammad's Call to be a Prophet

As a result of his religious feelings Muhammad began to spend time in prayer and meditation in cave Hira on Mount Nur. In particular he spent the whole month of Ramadan in prayer and contemplation and it was towards the end of Ramadan 610 CE (there is some dispute as to whether it was the 24, 25, 26 or 27) when the Lailat al'Qad'r (Night of Power and Excellence) occurred. This was when God sent an angel to Muhammad with the command to recite. This was the first revelation of the Qur'an to Muhammad and is found in sura 96, 'Read in the name of thy Lord and Cherisher who created, created man out of a mere clot of blood'.

Muhammad was terrified and ran home to Khadijah thinking he was going mad. She comforted him assuring him that he was not mad, but being called by God, 'her words of consolation were in response to the Prophet's apprehensions that under the impact of Divine Revelation either he would lose his reason or his life or be confronted with the tremendous responsibility that prophethood was to entail', (Ja'far Qasimi). She took him to Waraqa who confirmed that Muhammad was the prophet God had promised in the Christian Bible to send to the Arabs.

The Beginnings of Islam in Mecca

Later Muhammad received the second revelation, sura 74 *The Mantled One*, whilst at home resting under a blanket (mantle). This revelation ordered Muhammad to 'rise and warn' (though some scholars think this did not come till 612CE). At first he just did this among his family and close friends. The revelations continued and a pattern gradually emerged:

1   Meccan polytheism was wrong 'there is no God but God' (the beginnings of tawhid);

2   Muhammad was not being called to bring a new religion to Arabia, he was being called to bring Arabia back to the religion of Islam which was the original religion of Arabia (the beginnings of risalah);

3   the Arabs were to be judged by God on their religion and way of life, therefore they had better repent and change to a good life of honesty and concern for the poor (the beginnings of akirah).

As a result Muhammad, Khadijah and Waraqa began a system of morning and evening prayers facing Jerusalem during which they prostrated themselves as a sign of their submission to God. This impressed other members of the family and Ali (the ten-year-old son of Abu Talib whom Muhammad was looking after) and Zayd ibn Harith became Muslims. Muhammad's best friend, another trader called Abu Bak'r, became the first convert outside the family.

Over the next three years several young members of Muhammad's clan became Muslims and by 613CE, there were about 30 Muslims.

Muhammad's public ministry in Mecca

In 613CE, the Prophet received a revelation telling him to make the message more public, 'Proclaim what you have been ordered and turn away from the polytheists', (sura 15 v 94).

Whatever the exact sura, there was certainly a change of attitude in 613CE. Muhammad set up headquarters in the house of a young wealthy convert, al'Arqam, who was a head of clan and lived near to the Ka'ba. From this centre the message of Islam was given to the people of Mecca. The first place of prayer was set up in the courtyard of the house and classes in the new religion and in the revelations were held there every day.

According to tradition, Muhammad made many converts at this time but they were 'chiefly weak and poor persons'. Montgomery Watt claims this does not mean exactly what it says. The converts were young members of the wealthy clans, older members of the weaker clans, strangers to Mecca who were outside the clan protection or slaves.

Why persecution began

Such converts posed a threat to the Meccan leaders. If Muhammad could make himself leader of the young men of Mecca then he would eventually become leader of Mecca. Furthermore, there was a tradition that any man who developed a great reputation for wisdom should become leader and if Muhammad was accepted as Prophet, it would give him that claim as well. On top of this Muhammad was threatening the wealth of Mecca by saying that the idols were nonsense. Mecca made a lot of money through the pilgrimage in Dhu al'hijja, money they could ill afford to lose.

The persecution in Mecca

Consequently, a hostile campaign was begun against Muhammad and the Muslims. There were attempts on Muhammad's life; some of his

followers were tortured or killed by exposure to the midday sun; his
meetings were broken up by hooligans; people threw rubbish and
thorns outside the door of his house. The Muslims were strengthened
by the conversion of two great Meccan warriors at this time, the
Prophet's young uncle, Hamza, and Umar who came to kill
Muhammad for converting his sister and was converted instead.

The persecution became so bad that Muhammad sent 83 Muslims, plus
their familes, who were not supported by their clans to flee to
Abyssinia where they would be well treated by Christians.

As the Meccans now had no way of attacking Muhammad because of
their protection by the clan system (abu Talib protected Muhammad
even though he never became a Muslim), the Meccan leader, abu Jahl,
began a new policy - the boycott of Hashim. Apparently this boycott
was soon extended to the other clans who were members of the League
of the Virtuous and Muhammad was in great difficulties.

During this period Muhammad apparently received many of the
revelations about the previous prophets of God e.g. sura 12 Yusuf,
sura 71 Nuh, sura 14 Ibrahim. Each of these revealed how God's
prophets had been rejected by their people, but in the end the will of
God had triumphed.

From Boycott to the Hijra

In 619CE the boycott was lifted. Some Muslims think it was lifted
because of Muhammad's revelations about the prophets which were
spread around Mecca, Western scholars because of the detrimental
effect it was having on Meccan trade - though Abd al'Rahman Azzam
claims it was because non-Muslim members of the boycotted tribes
were suffering as well. It seemed Muhammad had been vindicated.
However, a double disaster then befell Muhammad - his wife
Khadijah died and his protector abu Talib died five weeks later.

He went to the nearby town of Ta'if thinking they would accept Islam,
but they rejected him and actually stoned him so that he was driven
out of the town bleeding. In the desert he was visited by jinn who he
converted to Islam, this confirmed that God was with him and that his
mission would eventually triumph (sura 72).

Muhammad returned to Mecca under the protection of one of the
weakest clans, but was forbidden from preaching openly in the city -

he could only make converts at events like the fairs of Ukaz outside the city limits.

It was in this period of grief and self-doubt that al'Miraj occurred. This was a journey by night from Mecca to Jerusalem and then to heaven itself where Muhammad met other prophets. It is mentioned in sura 17 v 1 but the details come from Hadith.

It was during Miraj that Muhammad was told to extend prayers from three to five times a day.

Things must have looked pretty bleak for Muhammad at this point. Initially after his call in 610CE he had made a big impact on Mecca but now he seemed to have no future. Muhammad's only chance of missionary activity was to preach at the nearby annual fairs and it was at one of these in 620CE that he met six men from Yathrib. Perhaps because of their close contact with Judaism and consequent awareness of the nature of prophets, these six were most impressed by Muhammad, and, in 621CE, five of the six returned with seven more interested inhabitants of Yathrib.

The situation in Yathrib was very different from that in Mecca. It was an agricultural oasis as well as a trading centre. It had been dominated by Jews, but it had been taken over by two Arab tribes which made alliances with the Jewish clans. These two tribes, the Aws and the Khazraj, had been fighting for leadership of the city, but the Battle of Bu'ath 618CE had ended in stalemate. It must have seemed to the 12 Yathribans who arrived at Ukaz in 621CE that Muhammad represented the best chance of success for their city. They made the first Pledge of Aqaba in which they agreed to serve none but the Prophet, worship God alone and lead moral lives. Muhammad sent Meccan Muslims (under the leadership of Mus'ab ibn Umayr) back to Yathrib with them so that the converts could be correctly instructed and more converts could be made. In 622CE the 12 returned with 63 converts who seem to have represented several groups in Yathrib. They made the Second Pledge of Aqaba in which they agreed to accept Muhammad as their political leader as well as their prophet.

M.A. Shaban claims that the Yathribans simply wanted the trading expertise of Muhammad and the Meccans to establish a Yathriban trading centre 'they were thus securing adequate Maccan expertise and paying for it.' The traditional biographies claim that the Yathribans recognised Muhammad as the coming prophet they had been told about by the Jews, 'By Allah this is surely the prophet with whom the Jews threatened us. We must not let them get ahead of us with him', (ibn Hisham quoted by Maxime Rodinson).

Why did Muhammad Leave Mecca in 622CE?

Some have suggested that it was a 'flight' of Muslims from Mecca to Yathrib, but the more correct term is 'emigration'. As soon as the Second Pledge of Aqaba was signed, it was clear that Muhammad would move to Yathrib, because the people wanted him to be their leader whereas in Mecca he could not even preach. The following are possible reasons for the emigration:

1 Muhammad saw the pledges by the converts from Yathrib as a sign from God that he was to leave.

2 The reaction of the Meccans when news of the Second Pledge leaked out (they tortured some of the converts and tried to stop Meccan Muslims leaving) seemed to confirm this view because if the Meccans were against it, God must be for it.

3 It must have been clear to Muhammad from the revelations he was receiving that Islam could never be just a religion. It had to be a complete way of life and it meant that politics had to be a part of religion, the opportunity to go to Yathrib as the political leader as well as the Prophet would give Muhammad the opportunity to show what Islam was really about.

4 Muhammad must have been worried about the safety of his followers in Mecca and he would be able to protect them in Yathrib.

5 He must have been desperate to be able once more to preach openly the revelations from God.

The Hijra 622CE

There is little doubt that Muhammad saw Islam as a community religion rather than an individual religion long before he left Mecca, but the way in which he left Mecca makes it clear that he was intending to use the opportunity presented by Yathrib in order to establish a Muslim community there.

Rather than going first himself (as he had done at Ta'if), he sent 70 of his Meccan followers with their wives and children to Yathrib, so ensuring he had a base there. This provoked the Meccans who could see that if Muhammad and his followers established a strong anti-Meccan community in Yathrib, that could play havoc with their trade. There are several stories of how Muhammad's life was threatened, and how he and Abu Bak'r (who accompanied him on the final escape) were only saved by God's help.

When Muhammad arrived in Yathrib (which from now on can be called Medina - a shortened form of Medina Nabi - city of the Prophet), he behaved in a very statesmanlike way to ensure that his community was accepted.

The main reason for the people of Yathrib needing Muhammad was 'the blood feud', which meant the original civil war between the Aws (plus their Jewish clans Banu Qurayza and Banu al'Nadir) and the Khazraj (plus their Jewish clan of Banu Quaynuqa) could never end. Someone had to end the blood feud system.

Muhammad had been accepted as Prophet by members of both tribes in Yathrib and his arrival in the city meant that it was now possible for a Muslim state, based on Muhammad and the Qur'an, to be established; this was why the Caliph Umar decided that this event marked the beginning of Islam proper so that the new year of 622CE became 1AH, the beginning of the Muslim era.

The Problems Muhammad Faced while in Medina

Although it seemed in 644CE that the problems of the Muslims were over in 622CE, that would not have been evident to Muhammad at the time. He was faced by the following problems in his attempt to follow God's command and re-establish Islam as the religion of Arabia.

1   How to deal with the problems of Medina and unite it into a single strong community. Muslim scholars divide the people of Medina at the time into *Muhajirun* (emigrants who came from Mecca with Muhammad), *Ansar* (helpers - Medinans who accepted Islam fully), *Munafiqun* (hypocrites who accepted Muhammad as the one who could settle disputes, but who only pretended to accept Islam, were jealous of the emigrants and who wanted to keep Medina for the Medinans), and the Jews.

2   How to deal with the city of Mecca, which was bound to attack Medina if Muhammad succeeded in making it strong.

3   How to convert the whole of Arabia.

It is impossible to separate totally each of these aims and the methods Muhammad used to solve them, as they were all intertwined and each affected the other.

Muhammad and Medina

As far as Medina was concerned, Muhammad first showed his approach to this problem by his decision about where to live. If he chose either an Aws or a Khazraj area, the other tribe would be offended. So, according to tradition, he let his camel choose for him. So he built a house in the area of a minor Khazraj clan to whom he was related. He ensured that this new house had a huge courtyard which could be used as a place of prayer by the whole of Medina.

Next he established the ground rules for the city. Some of this has come to us in *The Constitution of Medina* (the earliest Muslim document in existence - it dates from about 640CE, but some of its contents could be from 622CE). The document shows how Muhammad was only the leader of the Muhajirun clan and that each clan kept its own clan leader. However, all blood feud rights were given up to the whole community (umma). All the Muslim believers also had extra commitments - a) they had to help any believer of whatever clan if they were in tremendous debt; b) all believers owed each other aid and protection so that war could only be fought on a united front and any believer who was attacked had to be protected whatever his clan; c) they had to obey a common moral code.

In addition Muhammad was to be the arbiter of any disputes, 'Wherever there is anything about which you differ, it is to be referred to Allah and to Muhammad'; and no military expeditions could be organised without the Prophet's consent.

So the old Arabic system of political leadership based on tribe and clan was to a certain extent confirmed, but Muhammad was also challenging it in the way in which he had made himself the leader of a whole city and by basing that leadership on religion (which was traditionally subservient to politics) he was challenging the whole political arrangement of Arabia (which was based on tribe and clan rather than religion).

The Establishment of the Religious Umma

According to the biographies, Muhammad at first regarded the Jewish clans as his main supporters because they already believed in one God. However, when he talked to them about the Qur'an, they argued with him about the differences between the Qur'an and their scriptures and his assertion that Jesus was a prophet.

Revelations were then given which made Islam more Arabic and less Jewish. The Qibla was changed from Jerusalem to Mecca (sura 2 v136-147). Ibrahim was repeatedly referred to as a hanif (the only prophet to have this title) and a true Muslim rather than a Jew. Emphasis was placed on the way the Jews had rejected all their prophets so it was to be expected that they would reject Muhammad.

Connected with this was the fact that the chief hypocrite, Abd'al ibn Ubayy (who had been trying to make himself King of Medina before the arrival of Muhammad) was a supporter of the Jews. By acting against the Jews, Muhammad gained the support of the anti-Jewish clans whose leader Sa'd ibn Mu'adh, became a Muslim.

After the Battle of Bad'r (see below) all the Arab clans of Medina officially became Muslims, but the Jews insisted on keeping their separate religion. There were some individual incidents of fighting and assassination between Jews and Arabs (especially the Muhajirun who needed to take over some trade in Medina to make a living and were often in conflict with the Jews over markets) and after one of these Muhammad led his troops against the Quaynuqa Jews. They were allies of Abd'Allah ibn Ubayy who tried to get Muhammad to make an agreement with them. However, the Battle of Bad'r had weakened Ubayy's position and Muhammad ignored him. The Jews of the Quaynuqa were forced to leave Medina and went to the Jewish stronghold of Khaybar to the North, leaving their markets to be taken over by the Muhajirun. The other Jews remained but the constitution seems to have changed and they no longer had any rights.

Islam was now the religion of Medina and in the process Muhammad had moved from just being the prophet who arbitrated on disputes, to being the acknowledged leader (though the other clan leaders still retained their rights, it became impossible for anyone to go against Muhammad because of his religious and military prestige).

As a result of the deaths in the fighting between Muhammad and Mecca, the booty from the battles and the loss of trade due to fighting, new regulations were needed and the revelations of the Qur'an made it possible for Muhammad to spend the next two or three years making Medina a theocracy (state ruled by God).

Zakah was established so that widows and orphans could be provided for and the proceeds of war split up fairly. Polygamy was encouraged so that the widows remarried and became protected again (in this period Muhammad made several marriages which cemented his relationships with the Muhajirun - he married daughters of Abu Bak'r and Umar - and established alliances with surrounding tribes).

Inheritance rules were revealed and riba (lending of money at interest) and alcohol were banned. Ramadan was established as a fast month and laws were revealed about making contracts.

So by 628CE, Muhammad had established a truly Arab religion in Medina, he had united the people in a theocracy and reduced the Jews to a subservient minority.

Muhammad and Mecca

Clearly Mecca was not going to accept Muhammad's takeover of Medina. He posed a threat to the whole concept of Arab leadership for not only had he become leader of Medina without being a member of the chief tribe, but also his religion claimed to have supremacy over the whole of Arabia so that he was actually making a claim to rule Mecca as well. Consequently it was in Mecca's interests to prevent Muhammad from gaining control of Medina.

Muhammad used a combination of methods to ensure success against Mecca:

1   he made sure that the Muhajirun in particular were trained for war by organising *razzias* (raids on trading caravans which did not usually involve bloodshed) in the locality of Medina almost as soon as he arrived;

2   this was followed up by the various military methods he used first to defend Medina against Mecca and then to conquer Mecca itself;

3   perhaps his major method was the religious one, not only did Muhammad use missionaries to convert the Meccans but he made it plain by his actions that the Meccans had nothing to fear from Islam, indeed they had much to gain because the Qibla and the Hajj showed that Mecca was to be the centre of Islam.

This can be seen by looking chronologically at the relationship with Mecca 622 - 630CE.

Battle of Bad'r 624CE

Muhammad's raiding parties had had an effect on the trade of Mecca and so when a large caravan set off from Gaza to Mecca in February 624CE, the Meccan leader, Abu Sufyan, accompanied it with a force of 70 Meccan soldiers. It was a very rich caravan of 1,000 camels and Abu

Sufyan was determined to lead it past Medina as a show of Meccan strength. Muhammad would have lost prestige in Medina if he had allowed this to happen and so he gathered 300 Muslims, 86 Muhajirun, 214 Ansar, and set off to intercept them at the wells of Bad'r where they were likely to stop for water. Abu Sufyan learnt of the plan and sent to Mecca for extra help and abu Jahl set off with a Meccan force of 950 men.

In the ensuing conflict, the Muslims were totally victorious, many Meccans were either killed or captured, but the Muslims lost only 14 men.

The result, and the way Muhammad had organised the battle, showed the Muslims that God was behind them, 'It was not ye who slew them; it was God... God is He who makes feeble the plans and strategems of unbelievers', (sura 8 v 17,18).

Certainly this was how it was seen in Medina where many of the more hypocritical Muslims stopped supporting Ubayy and became real Muslims. Several of the tribes around Medina made alliances with Muhammad when they saw that he was able to stand up to Mecca.

In Mecca itself there was a realisation that Muhammad and Medina would have to be dealt with in a more serious way.

Battle of Uhud 625CE

By March 625CE the Meccans were able to launch a much more serious attack on Medina. With 3,000 men (including an expert cavalry force led by Khalid) they marched on Medina.

Muhammad prayed and was given a battle plan, but was betrayed by Abd'Allah ibn Ubayy who deserted the Muslims at a crucial point in the battle. As it says in sura 3 v 166, 'What ye suffered on the day the two armies met, was with the leave of God in order that He might test the Believers and the Hypocrites also... '

In the battle, Muhammad's (or God's) plan was initially extremely successful and the Meccan infantry was routed. However, when they saw this, the Muslims, whom Muhammad had ordered to stay on the hill whatever happened, left their posts to join in the end of the battle and Khalid then brought his cavalry in from the rear forcing Muhammad to retreat back up the hill. Muhammad himself was wounded, and the Medinans regarded this battle as a defeat.

In fact it was really a Muslim victory because the Meccans were not able to follow up their advantage. They left Medina to return to Mecca the same day leaving Muhammad in control of their trade route. This can be seen by the fact that it was two years before they were re-organised sufficiently to attack Medina again. Muhammad used this time not only to consolidate his military strength and tactics, but also to establish Islam more firmly so that there would be plenty of committed Muslims when the next attack came.

The Battle of the Trench (Battle of Ahzab) 627CE

In 627CE the Meccans gathered the largest army seen in Arabia for many years (10,000 men) and marched on Medina. This time Muhammad listened to a Persian convert, Salman, as well as praying for guidance. The crops were harvested before the Meccans arrived, and a huge trench was dug around the centre of the city with stakes in the trench so that cavalry could not cross it.

This type of warfare had never been used in Arabia before and the Meccans had no idea of how to deal with it. Their conventional attacks failed and their negotiations with the Jewish clan of Qurayza, who they wanted to attack from the rear, also failed and after a fortnight, they ran out of supplies and returned to Mecca.

The Treaty of Hudaybiya 628CE

Muhammad was now in a much stronger position and he made many more alliances with the tribes between Medina and Mecca.

Then in 628CE he had a vision of himself doing a pilgrimage to Mecca for God and so he gathered a Muslim army to march towards Mecca ready for the pilgrimage. It appears that he did not want to fight because when he was met by a Meccan army north of Mecca at Hudaybiya, he was quite ready to make an agreement with them. The terms of the agreement were:

1   the Muslims would not be allowed into Mecca in 628CE, but would be able to enter for three days in 629CE;

2   Meccans taking refuge in Medina would be handed over to the Meccans, but Muslims taking refuge in Mecca would not be handed over to Muhammad;

3   there would be a ten year truce in which Meccans and Muslims would be free to travel in Arabia;

4   each party would remain neutral in the event of a war between the other and a third party;

5   any tribe wishing to make an alliance with either Muhammad or Mecca would be free to do so.

At first sight this appears a diplomatic defeat for Muhammad, but it was extremely beneficial to him. Muslims who were kept in Mecca or who were forced to go back to Mecca converted many Meccans. Muslim missionaries were free to go anywhere in Arabia and many tribes were converted in the next few years. The pilgrimage in 629CE had a great effect on Meccan public opinion for it showed they would not lose any pilgrimage trade by becoming Muslim.

The Conquest of Mecca

So successful was Muhammad that when the Meccans broke the treaty in 630CE by foolishly attacking a tribe under Muhammad's protection, Muhammad was able to lead an army against Mecca. He wisely did not attempt to take Mecca by force immediately. Firstly, he camped outside the city and made converts of people like Khalid who came out to see him. Then he warned everyone to stay indoors whilst he entered the city with his army. Those who did not were fought against and 28 Meccans were killed. A number of Muhammad's greatest enemies were executed, but in the main an amnesty was declared and Mecca rapidly became Muslim.

Muhammad and the rest of Arabia

Muhammad's aim was the conversion of the whole of Arabia starting with the areas around Medina and Mecca. He did this initially by sending missionaries to talk about Islam; this was often followed up by an attempt to make an alliance (made easier as Muhammad's prestige grew) often cemented by a marriage between the clan leader's daughter and either Muhammad or a leading Muslim.

Muhammad seems to have been able to show that a clan would be better off under Muslim rather than Meccan protection especially in the years after 628CE. The only potential opposition was removed when the Jewish fortress of Khaybar was captured and the Jews made subject peoples.

After the conquest of Mecca, Muhammad was faced with a major problem as the central Arabian tribes of Hawazin decided to take advantage of the Mecca-Medina conflict to attack them themselves. This was repulsed at the Battle of Hunayn in 630CE and, thereafter, almost all the tribes of Arabia accepted the supremacy of Muhammad and Islam. Muhammad even sent an expedition to Tabuk on the edge of the Byzantine Empire.

However, it is likely from the later evidence that with the exception of the areas around Mecca and Medina, there was little real commitment to Islam, it was merely acknowledgement of the supremacy of Muhammad. This would explain why they deserted Islam when the Prophet died.

Nevertheless, Muhammad had successfully challenged the idea of tribal separation and leadership in Arabia. For the first time in its history, Muhammad had united Arabia behind one leader by making them acknowledge one religious faith.

The Death of the Prophet

In 632CE Muhammad made his final pilgrimage which gave the example for all subsequent pilgrimages. At Arafat he made his final sermon to 120,000 Muslims. The traditional text is in Sarwar pages 119 - 120 and contains these words, 'Oh people listen carefully! All the believers are brothers... none is higher than the other unless he is higher in obedience to Allah. No Arab is any superior to a non-Arab except in piety.'

When he returned to Medina from the Hajj, he caught a fever and had to allow Abu Bak'r to lead Salah for him. The fever left him momentarily and he led a last Salah just before he died.

There was much grief in Medina and many refused to believe Muhammad had died, it was left to Abu Bak'r to make the response of Islam to the Prophet's death, 'Oh Muslims, he who worshipped Muhammad should know that Muhammad is dead, but he who worshipped God should know that God lives and never dies.'

The Changes Muhammad Brought to the Way of Life in Arabia

It is important to note exactly how much of a change Muhammad and the religion he brought made to the way of life of the people of Arabia. Perhaps the best way to do this is to go through the Qur'anic religion and see what changes were imposed.

The Five Pillars must have imposed considerable changes.

The Shahada's insistence that 'there is no god but Allah' meant that all the forms of Meccan polytheism had to be abandoned. Idol worship in all its forms was banned. Admittedly, meat still had to be slaughtered in a sacrificial way, but it was the way of the Jews rather than the way of the Arabs.

Salah must have meant a major change from a religion with very few formal prayers to the five times a day ritual which also involved the erection of prayer places throughout Arabia. Presumably the regulations on wudu must also have meant a major change to a far from hygienic people.

Sawm was a major change in terms of the month long fast of Ramadan, but Ramadan had always been a sacred month in Arabia and the Jews and Christians had their fasts of Lent and Yom Kippur.

Zakah was in a sense a major change as it was the lack of concern for the poor and the greedy self-interest of the merchants which had aroused Muhammad's dissatisfaction. However, there is some evidence that the system of al'hums established by Hashim was based on a fair sharing of wealth, 'It was again Hashim who introduced another revolutionary measure.This was to give the poor some share in the profits', (M.A.Shaban).

Hajj was merely an 'Islamisation' of the ceremonies already associated with Mecca and Mina, though the confession at Arafat was probably added by Muhammad. Nevertheless, there were major differences in what the Arabs were expected to do on Hajj making them aware of the oneness of God and the brotherhood of Islam.

The possession of a holy book made another great change. The Jews and Christians had their holy books, now the Arabs had theirs and it was one which told them exactly how to change their lives. This was to be their guide book and the beliefs of tawhid, risalah and especially akirah would have been a great incentive for change.

It is not known how much of the Shari'a was established during the life of Muhammad, but it can be safely assumed that all the commandments of the Qur'an were in place. Therefore, the Meccans would have had to stop their drinking and gambling. Charging interest, eating pork etc. would have been things of the past. The whole attitude to marriage, divorce, the status of women, the killing of female babies were all revolutionised and there can be no denying the Muslim claim that Islam raised the status of women, 'If we... look into the position of the women in Islam, we must conclude that Islam liberated women from the dark age of obscurity fourteen hundred years ago', (Ghulam Sarwar).

However, it should be remembered that Muhammad never claimed to be introducing a new religion, he was simply bringing back Islam to the Arabs who had received it from Adam and Ibrahim, but then distorted it. Muhammad was simply removing the distortions,

> His religion was not new. He insisted it had always been there and it was no different from that of previous prophets beginning with Abraham. He was only calling for the restoration of a proper application of the principles of the eternal truth. This restoration would ensure justice and salvation for all his followers. Justice for all based on cooperation by all was the best guarantee for peace and prosperity, (M.A.Shaban).

Certainly Islam did not require any change in the Meccan way of life in terms of trading, 'God hath permitted trade and forbidden usury', (sura 2 v 275), but it must have meant considerable changes to the ordinary daily life of a Meccan.

The Significance of the Life of Muhammad for Muslims

For all Muslims the life of Muhammad is of the utmost significance. Muhammad was 'the Seal of the Prophets' who was given the final revelation of God in a way that could never be distorted. He renewed Islam in Arabia and established the first Muslim state.

He is therefore regarded as 'the great exemplar', the one whose life is the perfect example for all Muslims to follow. This can be clearly seen in the following quotations from Muslim authors,

> He practised meticulously what he preached. His character and demeanour had a magnetic quality about them. His conduct and behaviour impressed even his bitterest enemy. He had a superb personality. His life was a perfect example of total obedience to Allah's commands, (Ghulam Sarwar).

> Such was our Holy Prophet Muhammad (blessings of Allah and peace be upon him). He was a prodigy of extraordinary merits, a paragon of virtue and goodness, a symbol of truth... His life and thought, his truthfulness and straightforwardness, his piety and

goodness, his character and morals, his ideology and achievements - all stand as unimpeachable proofs of his prophethood, (Abul Ala Mawdudi).

The Sufi Ja'far Qasimi says,

> The inner substance of the Prophet is the hidden fountainhead of Islamic spirituality. This inner reality manifests itself in the life (sirah) of the person considered by Muslims to be the last prophet and the perfect man par excellence and also in his actions (sunnah) and sayings (ahadith). His beautiful names, which traditionally are said to be two hundred and one, are chanted in litanies and recited in certain spiritual exercises.

There are some Muslims (especially of the Wahhabi group who dominate Saudi Arabia) who object to these qualities which are attributed to Muhammad as they are elevating him beyond the human and so lead to the possibility of shirk. However, the vast majority of Muslims see Muhammad as the perfect example and try to follow his example in their lives.

The Sources for the Life of the Prophet

All this information concerning the Prophet comes from the biographies written by Muslim authors over a hundred years after Muhammad's death. These biographies often contradict each other and these notes are based on the accepted interpretations as found in both western and Muslim books.

The traditional biographies are ibn Ishaq 750CE (as translated by ibn Hisham in 800CE), Ma'mar ibn Rashid 750CE and al'Waqidi 800CE. There are considerable differences between these biographies and one example quoted by Michael Cook in his biography *Muhammad*, 1983, shows this quite clearly.

Referrring to when Abd' Allah died, ibn Ishaq says, 'Abd' Allah died while his wife was pregnant with Muhammad though it may have been when Muhammad was 28 months old - Allah knows best which is right'. Ma'mar ibn Rashid says that Abd'Allah most probably died whilst Muhammad was still in the womb and it happened at Yathrib where he had been sent by Abd'al Muttalib to buy dates. Two other ninth-century short biographies say that Muhammad was either in the womb, two or seven years old and again, 'Allah knows best which is right'. Waqidi says that Abd'Allah had been on a business trip to Gaza and fell ill on the way back; he stopped at Yathrib to be nursed by relatives and died there. Waqidi gives Abd'Allah's exact age at death and says that although there are other estimates as to how old Muhammad was when this happened, this is the true account.

Such problems have made some modern Muslims distrustful of the biographies and they believe that many of the incidents (such as Muhammad marrying Abu Bak'r's daughter A'isha when she was seven and he was 50 and the execution of the Jews of Qurayza) were inserted by later leaders (such as the Umayyad Caliphs who were not religious) in order to justify their own conduct.

There are some external sources for the life of Muhammad which have come to light more recently. They comprise: Greek and Syriac manuscripts from the 630s; an Armenian history of the 660s; a Hebrew apocalypse of the eighth century which contains an earlier apocalypse from the 630s; Arabic coins from the end of the seventh century.

These sources agree that there was a man called Muhammad who began a religion in Arabia in the early seventh century. The manuscripts refer to his followers as muhajirun and one manuscript from 643CE refers to the year 22 implying the Muslim dating system. The Armenian historian asserts that Muhammad was a merchant who became a prophet and that Abraham was the main figure in the monotheistic religion he founded.

However, there is no mention in any of these sources of the words Muslim, Mecca or Qur'an (except on the coins which are inscribed with Qur'anic verses - though these have some slight differences from the authorised Qur'an).

The early Greek sources claim that Muhammad was still alive in 634CE and that he took part in the conquest of Palestine. The Armenian historian asserts that Muhammad led a combined force of Jews and Arabs into Palestine. All these early sources claim that Muhammad was regarded as the Jewish Messiah and that his army was a mixture of Jews and Arabs which would imply that the traditional biographies are wrong about Muhammad's split with the Jews.

These external sources only came to light in the 1960s and 1970s and have not been the subject of much scrutiny, though they have revolutionised the approach of Western scholars to the biography of Muhammad,

> We have to consider the whole nature of the Islamic historical tradition... it is late, biased and, in its portrayal of early religious

developments, difficult to accept for anyone experienced in the comparison of historical and literary materials. That it should have been largely accepted for so long by orientalists is an extreme example of the results of overspecialisation in universities after the First World War, (Julian Baldick article in *The World's Religions*, Routledge, 1988).

However, Muslim authors still refer solely to the traditional biographies as does the latest Western biography of Muhammad by Karen Armstrong

CHAPTER SIX

A BRIEF HISTORY OF ISLAM

The Situation at the Death of Muhammad

Muhammad's struggle against Mecca had had a disastrous effect on the trade of Arabia which had been dominated by Mecca for about fifty years. Furthermore it is generally agreed by scholars (e.g. M.A.Shaban and M.Watt) that Arabia was still not actually Muslim. Muhammad had made alliances with the tribes of Arabia, but they had not all become a part of the Islamic umma. Indeed there is evidence of rival prophets among the tribes of Central Arabia (Musailimah and Sajah were the prophets here) and the Yemen (Aswad Ansi was the prophet there). The death of the Prophet, therefore, precipitated a crisis for the new Muslim state, as tribes which had only owed allegiance to Muhammad, not Islam, and tribes who saw a brighter economic future away from Islam, broke off their commitment to Medina.

These threats, however, did not only come from outside Medina. On the very day of Muhammad's death, the Khazraj met as a tribe to discuss their future. This was a major threat to the umma and so the Ulama (Muslim leaders in Medina) met immediately to decide on a policy. The problems they faced were:

1   How were the Muslims to be ruled ? The Qur'an implies that Muslims were to be ruled by God alone and the example of Muhammad seemed to be that the community was to elect religious men to be members of the Ulama who would interpret the laws given to Muhammad by God and now written in the Qur'an. The problem with this idea was that Muhammad had been the leader of the community whose decision would be final. Was there then to be a replacement for Muhammad (though essentially there could not, because Muhammad had been the final prophet)?

2   The wars between Mecca and Medina had totally disrupted trade and the economy of Arabia was collapsing. This seems to have occurred at a time of rapid population growth resulting in a need

to decide on the economic future of Arabia. Was it to go back to trade or expand the Arab dominated territory?

3   Then there was the problem of Islam itself. Was it the religion of the Arabs or was it a faith for the world?

These last two problems were dealt with by the rightly guided Caliphs, but the first problem has never been settled and some would say that it lies at the heart of current disputes in Islam.

Rightly Guided Caliphs

It was decided that a successor (Caliph or *Khalifa*) should be appointed to Muhammad. The principle was determined that the Caliph should be elected by the Ulama (which became a sort of electoral college) to carry on the work of Muhammad. The Caliph was not to take over from Muhammad, 'It was unthinkable that any ordinary man should wield the same powers as the Prophet', (M.A.Shaban), but simply to preserve the umma and follow the teachings of the Qur'an and Sunna.

Sunni Muslims regard the first four Caliphs (Abu Bak'r, Umar, Uthman and Ali) as 'rightly guided' (*rashidun*). In the Qur'an, Khalifa is used to mean 'successor of the blessings of the forefathers', and to Sunni Muslims, the first four Caliphs were successors to the blessings of the Prophet. This is because they were all muhajirun (Muslims who left Mecca with Muhammad in 622CE) who had been Muslims from the beginning and so could pass on Hadith. Furthermore, because they had known Muhammad so well, they were able to make decisions that were as binding as those of Muhammad himself.

For most Sunnis, this is the most important thing about the 'rightly guided Caliphs', they are the only ones whose edicts can be regarded as binding. They were the founders of the Islamic Empire who continued the work of Muhammad and so had God's guidance.

The Reign of Abu Bak'r 632 - 634CE

There is dispute among scholars about how much control Abu Bak'r had over the armies of Islam during his Caliphate, but it seems clear that under his leadership answers to the problems evolved.

Abu Bak'r sent an army to the border of the Byzantine Empire as Muhammad had wished despite the fact that Medina itself came under attack from the Ridda tribes (those tribes who deserted Islam and indeed turned against it). This move by Abu Bak'r demonstrated that Islam was to be a world religion and that the economic problems were to be solved by expansion.

It also showed that Abu Bak'r was operating from a position of strength and gradually the Ridda tribes were defeated. A particular success was when Khalid led his army against the Central Arabian Confederation (633 CE) and defeated them at the Battle of Aqraba. This brought about the collapse of the Ridda revolt (often called the Ridda Wars) and Khalid led his army against the nearby Sassanian Empire. The Sassanians were absentee landlords and Khalid was able to conquer the border territory relatively easily.

This brought cash into the Muslim coffers and Abu Bak'r authorised a campaign against the Byzantines led by Am'r ibn al'As. This was not as successful and Khalid was sent to help. After an incredible forced march across the desert (600 miles in five days) Khalid and Am'r defeated the full Byzantine army at the Battle of Ajnadayn in 634CE just before Abu Bak'r died.

The Reign of Umar 634 - 644CE

The Conqests of Umar

Umar had assisted Khalid in putting down the Ridda revolt, and now he seems to have been determined to allow a massive expansion of the areas under Medinan control. So far the advance had really only been on the edges of the great empires, but now Umar authorised wider attacks.

In the West, Syria was occupied and after the Battle of Yarmuk, 637 CE, Palestine was attacked and Umar himself entered Jerusalem in 638 CE. After this Muslim troops moved into North Africa until in 641 CE Umar called a halt on the Tunisian border.

In the East, after an initial setback against an army of elephants at the Battle of the Bridge, the Muslim armies pressed into Sassanian territory and at the Battle of Nihawand, 641 CE, the Sassanian emperor, Yezdigird III, was defeated and fled to India opening the whole empire to Muslim occupation.

So in the 11 years since Muhammad's death, the Muslim Arab armies had carved out an empire almost as large in size as that of the Romans.

The Organisation of the Empire

Such rapid conquest of such a large area left Umar with a major organisational problem. He solved it by:

1   establishing garrison towns on the edges of the conquered areas so that they could have rapid contact with Medina (Kufa, Basra, Damascus, Fustat - Cairo);

2   banning Arabs from buying land in the conquered areas;

3   keeping the current civil service in operation;

4   setting taxes on land related to whether or not it was owned by Muslims;

5   ensuring that non-Arabs who converted to Islam were treated as Arabs;

6   organising pensions for people in Medina and salaries for Muslim soldiers.

This system worked well, but in 644CE Umar was assassinated by a Persian Christian slave.

The Reign of Uthman 644 - 656CE

M.A.Shaban claims that there were major problems by the end of Umar's reign which are revealed by the fact that Umar appointed a *shura* of six prominent Muslims to decide what was to happen after his death. He claims that rather than this being an electoral college to determine the next Caliph, it was in fact to decide whether to continue with the Caliphate at all.

Eventually the Caliphate was offered to Uthman, after Ali had turned it down because of the problems.

The Conquests under Uthman

Uthman allowed the empire to spread westwards across North Africa and eastwards to the boundary of China and the Indus Valley in what is now Pakistan.

He also organised the first Muslim navy to protect Egypt from the

Byzantines and this managed to capture Cyprus and some of the Greek islands for Islam.

Uthman's Problems

1   Uthman had become leader of the Umayyad clan and was a very wealthy man. The Umayyads had been the main opponents of Muhammad in Medina, yet Uthman appointed his cousin Mu'awiya, who had fought against Muhammad at Uhud and the Trench, as Governor of Syria. Others of his relatives were given important positions as Uthman tried to bring the empire under his control. So competence rather than religion became the qualification for success.

2   The Muslim armies needed more men and so Uthman recruited the ex-Ridda tribesmen who had fought against Islam and Abu Bak'r. He also gave them the same salaries as original Muslim soldiers.

3   In the East the original Muslim warriors (known as the *Qurra* according to Watt because they were so religious and knew the Qur'an off by heart; according to Shaban because they came from the villages of Arabia) who had taken over the land deserted by the Sassanian rulers had it taken off them and given to a non-religious new governor.

4   Uthman seems to have been concerned that there were copies of the Qur'an with slight differences and that it was being passed down orally by remembrancers in their own dialect and so he ordered a copy to be made in the dialect of Quraysh (the Prophet's tribe), all other copies were destroyed and remembrancers banned. This alienated many of the pious.

As a result of these policies the Qurra from Iraq and Egypt went to Medina to protest and when Uthman refused to listen they attacked and killed him.

The Reign of Ali 656 - 661 CE

Ali was now the only candidate, but he never really had full control of the empire.

Two of the electors, Talha and Zubayr, organised a revolt based around the Prophet's widow A'isha. Ali defeated them when they arrived in Iraq at the Battle of Jamal 656 CE.

However, Ali faced a more formidable threat in the form of Mu'awiya who refused to recognise Ali until Uthman's murderers were brought to justice. It seems that Ali's supporters may have been involved in the murder, and eventually Ali and Mu'awiya met with their armies at the Battle of Siffin. This ended inconclusively (mainly because Mu'awiya's army put Qur'ans on their spears when they were being defeated so that the Qurra would not attack them) and Ali was forced to accept arbitration.

This caused the first schism as some of the Qurra said that as Caliph, Ali was the only arbiter and that by accepting arbitration he was admitting he was not the Caliph. They broke away from him and established the first independent Muslim state in Oman. They were called *Kharijites* (seceders) because they broke away from Ali and said that the Caliph should be the most religious man.

When eventually the arbiters came up with their decision, they were split. One said Ali was in the wrong and that Mu'awiya should be the Caliph, the other that Ali was in the right. However, before Ali could do anything about it, he was stabbed by a Kharijite whilst praying in the mosque during Ramadan 661CE.

Mu'awiya now took advantage of the power vacuum to make himself Caliph. He was obviously not sure of his support, however, because, although he bought Ali's eldest son, Hasan, off with a pension, he moved his capital from Medina to Damascus. The Qurra never accepted Mu'awiya and though he, and the Umayyad dynasty he founded, were in control of the empire until 750CE, the Qurra formed the Shi'a Ali (party of Ali) and organised its overthrow.

Why did Islam Spread so Rapidly?

It seems unbelievable that in the space of 25 years a group of Bedouin Arabs should come out of the desert and take over two of the most powerful empires in history. How did this happen ?

Traditional Muslim historians have a fairly straightforward answer to this very difficult question - it was because of the power and strength given by God, 'This unity of purpose made the Muslims a living force with initiative and drive; and when, having completed his mission, the Prophet of Islam passed away... they were the most disciplined people ready to take the word of God to every corner of the world.'
(M.A.Aziz)

More modernist Muslim historians and Western historians have discerned many other possible causes for Islam's success.

1   The Byzantine Empire was nowhere near as strong as it appeared. Syria, Palestine and Egypt were particularly disaffected. They had different languages from the Greek of Byzantium and they were being persecuted by the Orthodox Christian leaders because of their Monophysite Christian beliefs. Furthermore the Byzantines had imposed heavy taxes so that they had little support in these provinces.

2   Similarly the Sassanian Empire was moving away from the Iraqi heartland. The rule and language were Persian, whereas Iraq was Semitic. Much of the agricultural land was run by absentee landlords and the Persian religion of Zoroastrianism was not as popular as Nestorian Christianity. The ancient feudalism had just been overthrown by a military revolution and Iraq was feeling neglected.

3   Of even more crucial importance, the Sassanians and Byzantines had just ended a debilitating war in which they had lost the support of their Arab mercenaries. The Byzantine emperor tried to make his mercenary Ghassanid tribes convert from Monophysite to Orthodox Christianity. This failed and the Ghassanids deserted him, as a result of which the Sassanians invaded and captured Damascus and Jerusalem (614 CE). However, they then tried to convert their Lakhmid mercenaries from Christianity so losing their support and allowing the Byzantine emperor Heraclius to re-conquer the provinces by 628 CE.

4   Not only did this weaken the two empires, but it left Arab soldiers on the edges of the empires, who were disaffected and knew the military techniques of the empires.

5   Some nineteenth-century historians felt that overpopulation in Arabia and a drought forced the Arabs to leave. This is now being replaced by an economic argument

   Those who followed him (Khalid) were undoubtedly driven by their desire for any booty lying within the Sassanian domains. Such Arab forays had been a pre-Islamic practice... In fact they were now an economic necessity, not because of over-population in Arabia, but because trade, especially after the ridda wars, was in ruins. (M.A.Shaban)

6   Almost all historians are agreed, however, that the religion of Islam must have had a dynamic impact on the Muslim soldiers -

not least the Qur'anic teaching that soldiers dying on Jihad would go straight to heaven. Though there is much debate among Muslim scholars as to whether these wars were Jihads - there were certainly no attempts to convert any of the conquered peoples by force and non-Arab Muslims were treated as second class citizens by the Umayyads.

7   B.Lewis claims that Khalid and other Arab generals had mastered a new military technique of cavalry and rapid communication, and that the Arabs established their garrisons on the very edge of the desert for rapid communication (Kufa, Basra, Fustat and Damsacus), 'The strategy employed by the Arabs in the great campaigns of conquest was determined by the use of desert power, on lines strikingly similar to the use of sea-power by modern Empires... these garrison towns were the Gibraltars and Singapores of the early Arab Empire.' (Lewis)

8   The Arab conquerors were very clever in their treatment of the conquered peoples. Taxes were made lower than they had been. The civil service was retained. No land was taken off its owners (unless it had been owned by the government) and Christians and Jews were allowed to worship as they wished. As a result the Arabs were seen as liberators rather than conquerors, 'Therefore the God of vengeance delivered us out of the hand of the Romans (Byzantines) by means of the Arabs', (Syriac Christian author quoted by Lewis).

It appears that the Arab invasion could only succeed where there was a feeling of grievance against the current rulers.The early Muslims could not break into the Byzantine heartland, India or Europe beyond Spain.

Andrew Rippin in *Muslims: their Religious Beliefs and Practices*, Volume 1 (where he puts forward the view that Islam as it is known today was developed in the eighth and ninth centuries in a struggle between theologians and Caliphs) claims that the expansion was a political phenomenon which later used religion to justify what it had done, 'some of the most important evidence for making some distinction between the earlier and later roles and forms of the religion in the area comes from political actions of the early rulers of the conquered territory.'

A similar, but very different view was put forward by Sati al'Husri, an early leader of pan-Arabism, who claimed that the spread of Islam came after the Caliphate was established, not with it.

The Umayyad Caliphate 661-750CE

The first four Caliphs had been elected, but from the death of Ali onwards, the Caliphate became hereditary. Mu'awiya appointed his son as his successor and so founded the first Muslim dynasty of the Umayyads.

Under the Umayyads the conquest of North Africa was completed and Jebel Tariq invaded Spain (giving his name to Gibraltar) in 711CE. Spain was soon conquered and only the Battle of Poitiers in 722CE prevented the whole of France from coming under Muslim rule. In the East, Pakistan was reached in 712CE and western China by 750CE.

However, it was not all a one-way procss. Although Arabic took over as the language in most of the conquered territories, the Arab character of Islam was being changed as millions of non-Arab converts were made and brought Greek and Persian ideas into the religion.

The Umayyads were slow to realise the importance of this and although they eventually gave equal rights to non-Arab Muslims (*Mawali*), it was too late to prevent them from joining the Shi'a revolt against the Umayyads which led to their overthrow at the Battle of Zab.

The Abbasid Caliphate 750 - 1258CE

Bernard Lewis claims that the establishment of the Abbasid Caliphate was 'as important... as the French and Russian revolutions in the history of the West', because it marked a social and religious revolution. It was under the Abbasids that there was a flowering of Muslim culture with poets such as al'Mutanabbi, philosophers like al'Farabi, the theologian al'Ashari and the scientist and doctor Avicenna. Algebra, trigonometry, chemistry and scientific methods of navigation were all discovered as was the number system based on zero now used throughout the world.

However, the cultural advances were not combined with military and political advances. The Abbasids had never gained control of Spain which remained Umayyad and, in the tenth century, Egypt and North Africa became the independent Shi'a Caliphate of the Fatimids.

When the Seljuk Turks attacked Baghdad in 1050, they easily captured it and, though an Abbasid Caliph technically remained as ruler, the dynasty was really ended. Perhaps this is why the European crusaders managed to set up the Latin Kingdom of Jerusalem in 1099 before being defeated by the Kurdish Sultan, Saladin, in 1187.

The Middle Ages of Islam

In 1162 a warlord was born in Mongolia, by 1200 he had made himself Genghis (Lord Absolute) Khan (of the Mongols). By 1217, he had conquered China and then attacked the Muslim Empire. By the reign of his grandson Khublai Khan, the empire stretched from the Caspian Sea to the China Sea and from the White Sea to the Indian Ocean. (It was the threatened alliance between the Khans and the Pope which led to the opening of contacts between China and Europe and the first European travellers along the Great Silk Road.)

When it became obvious that Khublai and his descendants were more interested in China than their other Asian territories, there was a resurgence of Islamic culture and gradually five Muslim empires arose - the Uzbek in the Oxus-Jaxartes Basin; the Moghul in India; the Moorish in Spain and North Africa; the Safawid in Persia; the Ottoman in the Middle East.

These empires gradually extended their territories (though the Moorish was driven out of Spain in 1492 and gradually lost its North African territories to the Ottomans) so that by 1700 the Ottoman Empire ruled Romania, Bulgaria, Greece, Hungary, Yugoslavia, Albania, Turkey, Armenia, Syria, Georgia, Lebanon, Iraq, Jordan, Israel, Arabia and the Gulf States and most of North Africa; the Safawid Empire ruled Iran and parts of Afghanistan; the Uzbek Empire ruled the Muslim Republics of the former USSR and parts of China; the Moghul Empire ruled India, Pakistan, Bangladesh, Burma and Malaysia. Afghanistan, Mongolia, Indonesia and many African states also had Muslim governments.

These were the most civilsed and advanced areas of the world at the time. As W.C. Smith said of the Ottoman Empire at this time, 'Its armies won battles, its decrees were obeyed, its letters of credit were honoured, its architecture was magnificent, its poetry charming, its scholarship imposing, its mathematics bold, its technology effective.' More importantly, this was all done in the name of Islam, 'In Islam God had spoken, through it He was acting.'

Then towards the end of the eighteenth century, everything began to go wrong. The Uzbek Empire was gradually conquered by the Russians; the Moghul Empire was defeated by the British and after the war of 1856 was ruled by a Christian woman; the Ottoman Empire suffered its first defeat at the hands of Napoleon in Egypt and staggered from crisis to crisis until its final collapse in the First World War; the Safawid (though not actually conquered) was divided into 'spheres of influence' between the British and the Russians.

Islam in the Modern World

Whilst the Ottoman Empire survived, Islam had a political centre and focus of unity in the Sultan. However, since the collapse of the Ottoman Empire, Islamic politics have been trying to follow two contradictory principles:

1   a search for national identity following the European nation state principle;

2   a search for Islamic unity, for a quality with which Muslim states can identify and which will differentiate them from non-Muslim states.

The problems this contradictory approach has raised for Islam can be seen by looking at what has happened to Muslim countries since 1918.

1. The Arabic States

After the First World War, the Ottoman Empire was dismembered and Turkey was eventually established as an independent state at the Lausanne Peace Conference 1923. The first Turkish president, Kemal Ataturk (who had led the struggle for independence) tried to make Turkey a European state. European style laws were adopted, many Muslim customs were banned and after the Second World War, Turkey became a member of NATO. However, all the attempts to remove Islam from the political scene in Turkey have failed and during the 1980s there has been a growth of Islamic fundamentalism.

During the First World War, Britain had encouraged various Arab tribes to fight against the Ottomans on the promise of national independence. Unfortunately, Britain also encouraged the Jews of

Europe to fight and in 1917 issued the Balfour Declaration promising to establish a national homeland for the Jews after the war. Britain was left to deal with the consequences of these contradictory promises when the League of Nations made all the ex-Ottoman territories Mandates under the control of one of the victorious allies. Britain was responsible for Iraq, Trans-Jordan, Palestine, Egypt and Sudan. France was responsible for Syria and Lebanon.

As a result of Britain's promise, Jewish immigrants began to arrive in Palestine and with the rise of the Nazis and anti-Semitism, this soon became a deluge. In 1939 Britain restricted Jewish immigration to 75,000 a year, but this was soon circumvented by the various Jewish organisations involved in smuggling Jews out of Eastern Europe, and when the war ended, the Jews in Palestine decided to set up their own independent state. Faced by Jewish terrorist groups on the one hand and Palestinian Arabs determined not to give up their land on the other, the British simply left. In the subsequent war, the Jews managed to establish a small state which was quickly recognised by the United Nations and the State of Israel was set up in May 1948.

Israel was never recognised by the Arab states because the UN did nothing about the Palestinian Arabs being driven from their homes, and, indeed, many Palestinian Arabs are still in the refugee camps built for them in 1948.

In 1956 the new anti-Western President of Egypt (Gamal Nasser) nationalised the Suez Canal (which was jointly owned by Britain and France). This led to Britain, France and Israel invading Egypt in the Suez War. Although these three powers were militarily successful, it was a diplomatic blunder. The UN forced them to leave Egyptian territory and there was a great change in Arab politics. Revolutions took place in Syria and Iraq where the Ba'ath party took control. Gradually revolutionary governments took over in Libya, Algeria, Tunisia and the People's Republic of South Yemen. All of these governments had the following features: opposition to the existence of Israel; opposition to the West; national plans to industrialise as a means of relieving poverty. Several of the states were Muslim in name only and the Ba'ath parties of Syria and Iraq were actually dedicated to removing the influence of Islam on the country.

The division of the Arabic speaking Muslim states into revolutionary and reactionary (the monarchies of Saudi-Arabia, the United Arab Emirates, Kuwait, Oman, Morocco, Jordan) did not prevent them uniting against Israel in the Six Day War of 1967 and the Yom Kippur War of 1973. However, there have been increasing signs of disunity, seen first in the Camp David Agreement of 1978 (where Egypt agreed to recognise Israel in exchange for the return of the territories captured by Israel in the wars of 1967 and 1973) and more recently in the Iran-Iraq war and the Gulf War.

This failure of the Arab states to unite, or even to succeed in their only united policy of destroying Israel, has caused many Arab Muslims to see their salvation in radical Islamic fundamentalism rather than Arab revolution and all the Arab countries now have significant Islamic fundamentalist oppositions.

2. The Asian States

The two largest Muslim states are in Asia. Indonesia gained independence from Holland in 1949 under President Sukharno. However, when he tried to make the country communist, there was a military coup and since 1965, the communist party has been banned. Over 90 per cent of the country's 200 million plus population are Muslim, and although it has a pluralist democracy, there is a substantial Islamic fundamentalist party which wants to make Indonesia a fully Muslim state.

Pakistan was established as East and West Pakistan by the British when independence was given to India. This was the first modern state established by Islam, but it never really found a successful constitution and after the Civil War of 1971 East Pakistan became the independent Muslim state of Bangladesh.

In both Pakistan and Bangladesh there has been a struggle since 1971 between democrats and traditionalists and both countries now have growing Islamic fundamentalist groups.

Similar problems have affected the Muslim country of Malaysia.

Afghanistan demonstrated during the 1980s the dilemma of modern Islam. The Muslim freedom fighters managed to drive the atheistic Russians out of their country, but now the war continues as the various Muslim groups cannot decide on how the country should be ruled.

Many Muslims saw the Islamic revolution of 1979 in Iran as the way forward for Muslim countries. A despotic ruler who had ignored Islam was overthrown and a true Islamic state established. One of the great worries of the USSR was that this revolution would extend to the Muslim republics of the USSR. Now they have gained independence, it is indeed possible that more Islamic states will develop in Asia.

However, the Iranian revolution brought bloodshed in Iran and a war between Muslims in the long-lasting Iran-Iraq War of the 1980s. Iran has struggled with its constitution since the death of Khomeini and its intervention in the Lebanon was disastrous.

3. Islam in Africa

Islam conquered Egypt and North Africa during the time of the early Caliphs, and these countries are not only Muslim, they are Arabic speaking. It took a long time, however, for Islam to move South. It was during the sixteenth and seventeenth centuries that Islam moved into West Africa through the Sahara and East Africa through the trading settlement of Zanzibar. During the twentieth century, Islam has expanded rapidly in countries such as Ethiopia, Tanzania, Nigeria and Zaire. There is conflict in all these countries between Christianity and Islam and in the Sudan there is a civil war between the Muslim government and the Christian population in the South of the country.

Many Africans have welcomed Islam as a religion because of its non-Western character and its opposition to colonialism. Muslim missionaries are now active thoughout Africa.

4. Islam in the West

The Turkish invasions of the sixteenth and seventeenth centuries brought Islam into Albania and Yugoslavia, but it has been immigration brought about by the needs of industry, which has brought Muslims into Western Europe. France has about three million Muslims mainly from North Africa; Germany has about two and a half million Muslims mainly from Turkey; Britain has about one million mainly from the Indian sub-continent; Holland has about three hundred thousand mainly from Indonesia and Belgium has about two hundred thousand from North Africa and Turkey.

The United States has about three million Muslims some of whom are descendants of Muslim slaves brought over from Africa, but most of whom have emigrated to the United States during the twentieth century. However, it is in America that new westernised forms of Islam have developed recently such as the Black Muslim Movement and the Nation of Islam.

Conclusion

Islam is now so widespread, the ending of the Caliphate and rise of nation states has made it so diverse, that it is hard for Islam to present the united front which it did from its origins to the end of the Middle Ages. Nevertheless, the many Islamic fundamentalist groups around the Muslim World are trying to bring back that sense of Muslim community and brotherhood.

> The type of patriotism that should adorn Muslim youth is that he be a good example for the people of the homeland... In his service of his homeland and his people he must not, however, neglect Islam which has honoured him and raised him up by making him a brother to hundreds of millions of Muslims in the world. He is a member of a body greater than his people, and his personal homeland is part of the homeland of his religious community. He must be intent on making the progress of the part a means for the progress of the whole. (Rashid Rida)

CHAPTER SEVEN

DIFFERENCES IN ISLAM

Introduction

Although there are differences in certain areas between the four Law Schools, and cultural differences between Muslims of different nationalities, the major differences between Muslims concern the Shi'as and the Sufis.

The Shi'as constitute about 12 per cent of Muslims and differ from the Sunni majority because of their attitude to the descendants of Muhammad and rather different religious beliefs. Sufis are found in both the Sunni and Shi'a forms of Islam (but more frequently among the Shi'as) and are Muslim mystics who see Islam as concerned with a close relationship with God rather than with fulfiling the letter of the Shari'a and Pillars.

The Shi'as

The Reasons for the Emergence of the Shi'as

Both Sunni and Shi'a historians agree that Ali was Muhammad's first convert and constant companion. They even agree that Muhammad hinted on several occasions that Ali should succeed him as leader of the Muslim community. However, when the umma met to decide on the succession after Muhammad's death, political concerns appear to have taken precedence and Ali was not even invited to the meeting. Abu Bak'r was chosen simply because he was perceived as the only candidate who would be acceptable to the tribes of both Mecca and Medina because of his own lowly origins. Ali, as Muhammad's cousin and son-in-law, represented the Hashim clan which was unpopular in both cities.

As a result of the selection of Abu Bak'r, Ali retired from public life and helped neither Abu Bak'r nor Umar despite the fact that he had been one of Muhammad's chief generals.

Nevertheless, Umar appointed him as one of the six electors who were to select the third Caliph. However, Ali's known criticisms of the Caliphates of Abu Bak'r and Umar meant there was no way he could become Caliph when the other five electors insisted that there should be no change to the nature of the Caliphate. Consequently, Uthman was elected as successor to Umar.

Caliph Uthman was a member of the Umayyad clan which had been one of the chief opponents of Muhammad before 630CE. He appointed members of his clan as governors of the new provinces even though they had been opponents of Muhammad during his lifetime. Indeed his cousin Mu'awiya who was the son of Abu Sufyan was appointed to the chief post of governor of Syria.

In order to keep the armies going, Uthman allowed members of the Ridda tribes (the ones who had fought against Islam after the death of the Prophet) to become full soldiers and at the same time removed the privileges of the Qurra (the original soldiers of Islam who had settled in Iraq).

Uthman ordered the authorised Qur'an which meant he banned the official remembrancers who were very holy, pious Muslims, and this annoyed many of the religious Muslims.

All these facts made the Qurra feel that Uthman was betraying Islam and they revolted against their Umayyad governor and marched on Medina to present their grievances to Uthman. When he would not listen to them, they killed him.

Ali, was now the only candidate for the Caliphate and was elected in 656CE. Unfortunately Ali had many opponents. Two of the most prominent Companions of the Prophet, Zubayr and Talha, objected to a younger man becoming Caliph, and joined forces with A'isha (the Prophet's widow) who had a long-standing grudge against Ali. They formed an army and marched on Ali who defeated them at the Battle of Jamal 656CE.

Ali then made a major mistake in moving his headquarters from Medina to Kufa in Iraq allowing Uthman's cousin, Mu'awiya, to lead opposition based in Syria and the Hijaz (area around Medina). Mu'awiya used the pretext of Uthman's killers not having been brought to justice to start a civil war. During this war the inconclusive Battle of Siffin was fought and Ali was forced to accept arbitration.

In 661CE, perhaps because Ali had accepted arbitration, Ali was murdered by one of the Qurra. Mu'awiya took advantage of this to declare himself Caliph in Damascus and offered a pension to Ali's eldest son (grandson of Muhammad), Hasan, who stayed in Medina.

The Qurra of Iraq never really accepted Mu'awiya and when he died they invited Husayn (Ali's younger son and also a grandson of the Prophet - Hasan had now died) to come to Kufa and be their Caliph. Husayn set off from Medina with his wife and family and about 60 armed supporters. Mu'awiya's son, Yazid, thought Husayn posed a major threat and so he sent an army to intercept Husayn. They met at Karbala and when Husayn refused to turn back, he and most of his followers were killed.

The Qurra never accepted the Umayyads and they formed themselves into Shi'a Ali (the party of Ali). They formed secret societies throughout Iraq and were particularly successful in converting the Mawali (non-Arab Muslims who were not given equal rights by the Umayyads).

As the Umayyads became more and more unpopular, the Shi'a became stronger and in 750CE they overthrew the Umayyads at the Battle of Zab and established a Shi'a Caliphate, the Abbasids.

The Shi'a Imams

The vast majority of Shi'as are known as *Twelver Shi'as* because they believe that between 632CE and 873/4CE there were 12 Imams (successors of Muhammad) who were direct descendants of Ali and Fatima.

It is difficult to give precise historical details of these Imams because their biographies were written by Shi'as who were trying to prove things about Imams.

> Among the specific points that Shi'i writers sought to prove about each Imam were: that their births were miraculous; the baby Imam being born already circumcised and with his umbilical cord already severed; that they spoke immediately on birth (and sometimes from within their mother's womb); that each was specifically designated by the previous Imam (or in the case of Ali by Muhammad); that each performed miracles and was possessed of supernatural knowledge. (Moojan Momen)

Ali the first Imam 632 - 661CE

Ali's Imamate has already been described, but it is important to realise how he is viewed,

> Ali... has assumed, even in the eyes of Sunni Muslims, an almost legendary dimension as a paragon of virtues and a fount of knowledge. His courage in battle, his magnanimity towards his defeated opponents, his sincerity and straightforwardness, his eloquence and his profound knowledge of the roots of Islam cannot be questioned for they are matters of historical record. He is also attributed with having been the founder of the study of Arabic grammar... and the originator of the correct method of reciting the Qur'an. His discourses and letters... are considered the earliest examples of Muslim writings on philosophy, theology and ethics. For Shi'as, the brief period of his caliphate is looked upon as a Golden Age when the Muslim community was directed, as it always should be directed, by the divinely chosen Imam. (Moojan Momen)

Ali was buried at Najaf in Iraq which is now a Shi'a holy city.

Hasan 661 - 669CE

Ali's eldest son was acclaimed Caliph on his father's death, but his only real support was the army of Kufa which had already let Ali down at the Battle of Siffin and which now had mass desertions when Mu'awiya approached with the army from Syria. Shi'as believe that Hasan gave up his rightful claim to the Caliphate to avoid useless bloodshed and that he spent the rest of his life studying Islam.

Husayn 669 - 680CE

The Shi'a believe that Husayn deliberately chose death at Karbala in order to show Muslims that force of arms is not enough to serve Islam, what is needed is sacrifice and suffering in order to change the hearts and minds of people. 'The martyrdom of Husayn has given to Shi'a Islam a whole ethos of sanctification through martyrdom.' (Moojan Momen)

Ali Zaynul Abidin 680 - 712CE

Ali was the only son of Husayn to survive Karbala. After Husayn's death, there were several Shi'a revolts, but they were based on other relatives of Ali. The fourth Imam kept out of politics and developed a reputation as a very holy and pious Muslim.

Muhammad al'Baqir 712 - 735CE

Muhammad's mother was the daughter of Hasan, so he combined the two lines coming from Ali. However, during his Imamate his half-brother Zayd claimed the Imamate on the basis that any descendant of Ali and Fatima who was learned and pious could put forward a claim. Zayd had studied under the founder of the Mu'tazilites (see chapter one). He gained many followers, especially when he accepted several Sunni ideas and agreed that Abu Bak'r and Umar had been rightly guided. However, this lost him the support of the true Shi'a especially when Muhammad al'Baqir emphasised the doctrine of the *nass* (the designation of an Imam by the previous one). Nevertheless, there are still Shi'a sects based on the Imamate of Zayd.

Jafar as'Sadiq 735 - 765CE

Jafar had the greatest reputation for scholarship of the Imams. He was a famous teacher and Malik and Hanifa (the founders of the Sunni law schools) were his pupils. The Umayyads left him alone to teach in Medina, but the arrival of the Abbasid Caliphate meant trouble for the Imams. The Abbasids claimed their right to the Caliphate through the Prophet's uncle, Abbas, and so the descendants of Ali and Fatima were bound to pose a threat to them. Consequently, Jafar was frequently imprisoned by the Caliphs. It was Jafar who developed the doctrine of *ilm* (the special knowledge of the Imam) and *taqiyya* (the right to pretend to be another religion if you are going to suffer for being a Shi'a).

Musa al'Kazim 765 - 799CE

During the earlier years of Musa's Imamate there was great confusion over who was the Imam. It was claimed that Jafar had appointed his son Ismail and when Ismail died before Jafar, he then appointed Ismail's son Muhammad. However, many Shi'as believed that Jafar could not have appointed Ismail because his supernatural knowledge would have meant that he knew Ismail would pre-decease him. So they accepted the claim of Ismail's younger brother, Musa.

Most of the extreme Shi'a sects come from those who accepted Ismail's Imamate.

Towards the end of his Imamate, Musa became more popular and as a result was executed by the Abbasid Caliph.

Ali ar 'Rida 799 - 818CE

Ali was the first Imam to be designated as a successor by a Caliph. It was while he was at the court of the Caliph Ma'min that his saintly sister, Fatima, came to see him and died at Qom in Iran. Her shrine there made Qom a holy city and it is now the centre of theological study in Iran.

Unfortunately, Ali died before he could succeed to the Caliphate.

Muhammad Attaqi 818 - 835CE

Muhammad was only seven when his father died. He was, however, very clever and at the age of 15 was married to the Caliph's daughter. Muhammad died shortly after the Caliph and Shi'as claim he was murdered because of his claim to be the next Caliph.

Ali al'Hadi 835 - 868CE

He was only six when he succeeded as Imam, and was relatively free until Mutawakkil became Caliph in 847CE, when he summoned Ali to Baghdad and placed him under house arrest in Samarra until his death in 868CE. During this time he kept in touch with his followers through secret messengers.

Hasan al'Askari 868 - 873/4CE

He was born in Samarra and lived all his life in semi-captivity. Again he kept in touch with his followers through secret mesengers.

Muhammad al'Mahdi (Al'Muntazar) 874CE

Hasan's brother claimed the Imamate on his death, as Hasan was thought to have had no children. However, a young boy appeared at Hasan's funeral and led the prayers. Twelver Shi'as believe he then went into hiding in a cave under the mosque of Samarra from where he will emerge as the Mahdi to bring in the end of the world and the Day of Judgement.

After he went into hiding, there were four men who claimed to be *Babs* (gates) who had direct contact with the Hidden Imam and gave his messages to the Shi'as. This period is known as the 'Lesser Occultation' (becoming a spirit in hiding). The last Bab died in 941CE since which has been the time of the 'Great Occultation'. The life of the Hidden Imam has been miraculously extended and he is still in control of the affairs of men and communicates through the dreams of holy men.

The Subsequent History of the Shi'as

The Abbasid Caliphate never ruled the whole of Islam, and the

Abbasids mark the end of the united Muslim empire. Spain and Portugal were still ruled by an Umayyad Sunni Caliphate. Gradually the Abbasids themselves realised that Shi'ism was too minor a religion ever to unite the Muslim Empire, and they gradually became more Sunni. When they became Sunni, they moved their capital to the new city of Baghdad which they used to subjugate Shi'as. Many Shi'as fled eastwards to Iran and Pakistan, but substantial numbers stayed around the Shi'a holy cities of Karbala and An'Najaf.

Although a small Shi'ite kingdom remained in Yemen and on the the shores of the Caspian Sea, Shi'a Islam did not again achieve any sort of power until the Safawids took over Iran in the sixteenth century. Since then Iran has remained the only fully Shi'a country and has close links with the Shi'a community in Iraq (probably over half the population despite the fact that Iraq is ruled by Sunnis - though Saddam Hussein's Ba'ath party is dedicated to making Iraq a secular state).

Shi'as total about 90 million around the world (800 million Sunnis). The main Shi'a centres are:- Iran (90%), Iraq (57%), Azerbaijan (55%), Bahrein (55%), Kuwait (40%), Lebanon (30%), Afghanistan (35%), Qatar (20%), Turkey (15%), Pakistan (15%), Saudi Arabia (5%), India (2.5%, but 8 million people).

The Beliefs of Shi'as which Differ from Sunnis

1   **The Imam** - The figure of the Imam is totally different. In Shi'ism, the Imam is a semi-divine figure who is a successor of Muhammad and must be a descendent of Muhammad. The Imam can commit no sin and is an intermediary between man and God. Every Imam is designated by the previous Imam thus ensuring continuity (the doctrine of nass).

Shi'as differ as to how many Imams there have been. The main group of Shi'as, Twelvers, believe that there were twelve descendants of Muhammad who were given the divine light by God. The twelfth (Muhammad al'Mahdi) went into hiding and will return as the Imam Mahdi to bring in the end of the world.

Other Shi'as believe that the fifth Imam Zayd was the last and that he went into hiding. Others believe that the seventh, Ismail, went into hiding.

However, all Shi'as agree that Muhammad appointed Ali as his successor and gave Ali the divine light so that Ali had God's power to decide what Muslims could and could not do. This power was passed from Ali to his son Husayn and then to his son etc.

2   **The powers of the Imam** - Clearly from what Shi'as believe about Imams, their powers must be considerable. The Imam is the one who determines what the Qur'an means and who determines what the law should be - the problem is to know what the Imam says! There is a Shi'a Hadith which says, 'whosoever knows not the Imam of his age dies the death of a heathen.'

Shi'as have two views on this: a) specially chosen descendants of the Prophet keep in touch with the Hidden Imam and pass on his wishes to the community (this is mainly found among Ismailites e.g. the Agha Khan is supposed to be a descendant of the Prophet and is the leader of a Shi'a group called the Khojas); b) specially able religious leaders who have gone through complex training in a holy city (e.g. Qom in Iran) become *mujtahids*. Leading mujtahids are known as *ayatollahs* (sign of God) and some believe that the Hidden Imam chooses one ayatollah as the leading authority - though many Shi'as believe that new messages can only be given by all the ayatollahs working together.

There is also a belief that the Hidden Imam sends a renewer (*mujaddid*) every century to revitalise Shi'ism. A task performed for the fifteenth Muslim century by Ayatollah Khomeini.

3   **Attitude to the rightly guided Caliphs** - All Shi'as believe that Abu Bak'r, Umar and Uthman knew that Muhammad had appointed Ali as his successor and deliberately kept quiet about it. Therefore, Shi'as regard the first three Caliphs as the great traitors of Islam rather than the rightly guided. They are publicly cursed in Shi'a Juma prayers.

4   **Attitude to the Qur'an** - Shi'as do not believe in the eternal Qur'an they believe the Qur'an was created by God. They also believe that everything in the Qur'an has a hidden meaning which needs interpreting by religious leaders.

Some Shi'as believe that the Qur'an is not final and that it can be added to by the Imams and that it was altered by Sunnis so that references to the Twelve Imams were missed out.

5   **The Shahada** - Shi'as add to the Shahada 'and I bear witness that Ali was the friend of God'.

6   **Salah** - The Shi'as think the forehead should be prostrated onto

dust or earth or, preferably, a block of baked mud from Karbala.

Most Shi'as do not regard Juma prayers as obligatory in the Mosque, though this has changed in Iran since the Islamic Revolution.

7   **Sawm** - Shi'as fast in the same way as Sunnis but their fast is longer as it ends after the sun has completely set. Shi'as also spend three days of Ramadan mourning Ali who was martyred on 20 Ramadan.

8   **Zakah** - In Sunni countries this is paid to the state, but Shi'as pay it to their mujtahid. Shi'as also impose a 20 per cent tax on all savings which is also given to the mujtahid.

9   **Hajj** - Although Shi'as are expected to go on Hajj to Mecca, they also make pilgrimages to Shi'a shrines such as Karbala and Najaf. Shi'as believe that they get grace (*berakah*) from visiting the tombs of Shi'a saints.

10   **Tawhid** - Shi'as adopt a Mu'tazilite position and so do not accept that God has any physical attributes. They believe that Qur'anic verses which imply this must be interpreted allegorically.

Many Sunnis think that Shi'as do not really believe in tawhid because of their attitude to Imams and especially the Hidden Imam.

11   **Risalah** - Although theoretically Shi'as believe in Muhammad as 'the Seal of the Prophets', their beliefs about the Imams make it very difficult for them to believe this practically because they believe that there have been other messengers who have brought new messages.

12   **Akirah** - Shi'as differ from the Sunnis in the position they give to the Hidden Imam as the Mahdi rather than Isa who Sunnis believe is named as the Mahdi in the Qur'an. Many Shi'as also believe that faith in the atoning death of Husayn will bring them salvation from their sins and therefore heaven, rather than hell, on the Day of Judgement.

13   **Extra festivals** - The Shi'as have several festivals which are not celebrated by Sunnis. The main ones are: *Ghadir Al' Khum* which celebrates the appointing of Ali as Imam by Muhammad at the pool of Khum; *Al'Ashura* which celebrates the death of Husayn at Karbala.

Al'Ashura is the major festival of Shi'ism and takes place

annually at Karbala and throughout the Shi'a world. It is a time of great weeping and self-mutilation as Shi'as remember the betrayal and death of the second Imam, Husayn. There is often a passion play during which the Shi'a idea of being able to get to heaven by faith in the atoning death of Husayn is brought out. This is very similar to some Christians' attitude to the death of Jesus and is totally opposite to the belief of Sunnis, especially as it seems to involve an element of shirk in that prayers are offered to Husayn.

14   **Shi'a law** - The Shi'as have the same concept of Shari'a as the Sunnis and have Qadis to adminstrate the law. Often the Shi'a Shari'a is the same as the Sunni, but it has a fundamental difference in that the Hadith of Ali are to be consulted as well as the Hadith of Muhammad and if nothing can be found in Qur'an or Hadith, then the law is determined by the religious leader who is believed to be in contact with the Hidden Imam.

There are many differences between Shi'a and Sunni laws e.g. a) Shi'as are not allowed to eat meat prepared by Jews or Christians even though it is not haram food; b) Shi'as are allowed temporary marriage (a *muta* marriage is a marriage for a set period of time for a set amount of money); c) Shi'as are allowed to pretend to be either Sunnis or Christians if this will prevent them from being persecuted (taqiyya).

15   **Freedom and predestination** - Officially Shi'as do not believe in predestination. They accept the teachings of a group of Sunni scholars who were later declared heretical (the Mu'tazilites) that God cannot be responsible for evil and, therefore, humans must have free will and be independent of God's authority in this life. So Shi'as believe it is up to the individual Shi'a as to whether they follow the Shari'a etc. However, this does not mean that Shi'as will not enforce the Shari'a.

16   **Attitude to the Government** - Shi'as believe that the only real government is through the Imam. However, until the Mahdi comes, a monarchy or rule by a religious leader with a reputation for piety is the best form of government. There is no real concept of democracy among Shi'as because authority rests with the Hidden Imam. The ordinary Shi'a obeys the Shari'a and any extra rules laid down by the mujtahids. This has caused major problems in Iran.

Everyone was in agreement that they wanted an Islamic government, but there was no consensus as to what an Islamic government was. Khumayni's concept... was that the constitution and law of the country is already determined by the Islamic Shari'a and only requires interpretation by the mujtahids and a planning council, also under clerical control, to determine priorities. There was really no place in Khumayni's original scheme for any political parties, parliament or other democratic elements. (Moojan Momen)

Shi'a Sects

Although Twelver Shi'ism makes up the vast majority of Shi'as, there are many sub-groups and sects, some of which would not be accepted by Sunnis as Muslim. This is particularly true of the various Ismaili sects. The Druze, for example, believe in reincarnation, they do not see the need to observe the Pillars and claim that the Fatimid Caliph, al'Hakim, was God. The Nizari Khojas (led by the Agha Khan) believe that the Imamate continued from Ismail to the present day and that there is no Hidden Imam.

It was out of Ismaili Shi'a sects that the Ahmadiyya of Pakistan arose basing themselves on the teachings of Mirza Ahmad who claimed to be a reincarnation of Khrishna, Jesus and Muhammad with a message for the twentieth century.

The Bahai religion developed in Iran from the teaching of the Bab who claimed in the nineteenth century to be a new gate to the divine light.

The Sufis

Origins of Sufism

In some ways the Sufis are similar to the Shi'as. They too originated in the East of the Arab Empire. They too reacted against the materialism and lack of piety among the Umayyad Caliphs.

However, they are different from the Shi'a because they are not concerned with historical origins. They regard the first three Caliphs as rightly guided (rashidun) and look to their example as well as Muhammad's for how a Muslim should live: 'As for Muhammad, he bound a stone upon his belly when he was hungry; Abu Bak'r had a simple garment tied with two pins; Umar lived on bread and olive oil; Uthman was like one of his slaves in appearance.' (Sufi Hadith quoted by R.A.Nicholson)

From these ideas about the lives of the early Muslim leaders as compared with the luxury and wealth of the Umayyads, there arose a group of Muslim ascetics who were determined to make Islam a more devoted religion. Out of their asceticism, there gradually grew a Muslim mysticism in which Muslims could go into trances, have visions etc.

> The term Sufism, which has become over the ages very popularly used, and often with a wide range of meanings, originates from three Arabic letters sa, wa and fa. There have been many opinions on the reason for its origin from sa, wa and fa. According to some the word is derived from safa which means purity. According to another opinion it is derived from the Arabic verb safwe which means those who are selected. This meaning is quoted frequently in Sufi literature. Some think that the word is derived from the word saf which means line or row, implying those early Muslims who stood in the first row in prayer or supplication or holy war. Yet others believe that it is derived from suffa which was a low verandah made of clay and slightly elevated off the ground outside the prophet Muhammad's mosque in Medina, where the poor and good-hearted people who followed him often sat. Some assume that the origin of the word Sufism is from suf which means wool, which implies that the people who were interested in inner knowledge cared less about their outer appearance and often took to wearing one simple garment all the year round which was made of wool. Whatever its origin, the term Sufism has come to mean those who are interested in inner knowledge, those who are interested in finding a way or practice towards inner awakening and enlightenment. (Shaykh Fadhlalla Haeri)

The Principal Teachings of the Sufis

A Muslim who wishes to become a Sufi must attach himself to a Shaykh (often known in Asia as a *Pir*). The Shaykh will be a proven Sufi and many of the great ones from the past are associated with miraculous healings (sick Muslims will often visit the graves of famous Shaykhs to be healed).

The Shaykh will then teach him various techniques (*maqam*) to become a Sufi. They include such things as poverty, solitariness, silence, contentment, abstinence and thankfulness.

Eventually the disciple should attain the Sufi state (*hal*) where he passes away into God (*fana*) and will be so filled with the love of God that nothing else matters.

A Sufi once described fana as,

> He (God) makes them absent from this world when they are in union with Him... thereafter the souls of them that have known God seek after the verdant pastures, the beautiful vistas, and every lovely thing in this world consoles them for the loss of the artist's own presence. (Rumi, a famous medieval Iranian Sufi)

Often poetry, music and dancing (which are frowned on in the rest of Islam) are used to assist in achieving the mystical state.

> Sufism is primarily concerned with the heart that reflects the truth which exists within it, beyond time and in time. The Sufi is the whole human being. He recognises that his reality is beyond time and space, and yet he understands that he himself is caught in his body in order to experience the duality of time and space in this world. The Sufi is the one who realises the courtesy due to the prison of his body which has been given to him on loan for a few years. He is aware of the fact that he is returning to the abode of infinite bliss from which he originally emerged. Sufism is an art of beingness through the attainment of divine knowledge. It is not an intellectual exercise for scholarly investigations and post-graduate study. (Shaykh Fadhlalla Haeri)

How Sufism Relates to the Rest of Islam

It can be easy for Islam to become a legalistic religion where a Muslim simply follows the Qur'an, performs Salah, fasts in Ramadan, pays Zakah, goes on Hajj and observes the Shari'a without ever actually having any religious experience; without feeling near to God or having any religious joy. Sufis have tried to show Muslims that the heart of Islam is not the practices of the faith but the relation of the individual to God. As one of the greatest Sufis, al'Ghazzali, said,

> It is not enough to observe the law and rituals of Islam and to have a doctrine one is ready to defend against all-comers. A humble soul may be religious even though ignorant of theology

and Qur'anic interpretation. The core of religion is to repent of
one's sins, purge the heart of all but God and, by the exercises of
religion, attain a virtuous character.

So Sufis encourage Muslims to look at their relationship with God and
their religious experience rather than just obeying the rules.

Of course, this can cause problems in that the teachings of the Sufi
brotherhood (a group of Sufis using the same techniques and having a
common founder) can become more important than the Qur'an and
some Sufis have even recommended the ignoring of the Five Pillars !

Sufism is very popular in the poorer parts of the Muslim world where
the Sufi brothers offer people living in wretched conditions a glimpse
of a beautiful eternity lying before them. It is also proving a more
attractive form of Islam to Westerners and several universities
(especially in the United States) have Sufi groups.

CHAPTER EIGHT

ISLAM IN BRITAIN

Islam came to Britain in a variety of ways. The early Muslims came through trade and in particular the sea. There have been Muslim communities in South Shields, Cardiff, Liverpool and London since the 1880s. However, these early groups of Muslims were small in number and had little noticeable effect. Then in the 1950s, large groups of Muslims began to enter Britain from South Asia as a result of the shortage of labour in Britain. With the passing of the various Immigration Acts of the Sixties, the immigration became that of dependants, and the current situation is that most Muslims living in Britain have been here for some time or have been born here.

In the 1981 census 37 per cent of Muslims were born in the UK compared with 1.2 per cent in the 1961 census. It is likely that in the 1991 census, that figure will exceed 50 per cent.

The Muslim community is dominated by Muslims from Pakistani and Bangladeshi origins as can be seen in this table of the origins of British Muslims in the 1981 census:

Pakistanis/Bangladeshis	360,000
Indians	130,000
Turkish Cypriots	60,000
Arabs	50,000
East Africans	27,000
Malaysians	23,000
Iranians	20,000
Nigerians	15,000
Turks	5,000

('Islamic Communities in Britain', J.S.Neilsen, in P Badham *Religion, State and Society in Modern Britain*)

These figures are not likely to be completely accurate, but they reveal the fact that the Muslim population of the UK is very mixed culturally which is perhaps why it is difficult for it to present a united front.

Cultural Differences in the Muslim Community

It is often not appreciated by non-Muslims that Muslims from different cultures will have different practices even though they are all Muslims. For many British people Muslim equals Pakistani.

In fact Muslim countries have different cultures just as Christian ones do. In particular Pakistani, Indian and Bangladeshi Muslims often observe *Biraderi*. This is similar to the Hindu concept of caste, but is based on wide familial ties. Many Asian Muslims will only marry someone from the same Biraderi. This is cultural and is quite against the Muslim teaching of the brotherhood and community of Islam. Attitudes to dress, marriage customs etc. are all matters of culture and can be causes of division in the British Muslim community because individual Muslims think they are part of Islam rather than part of their national culture.

Most mosques are organised for nationalities i.e. there will be a Pakistani mosque, a Bangladeshi mosque etc.

Other Divisions in the British Muslim Community

As well as national ethnic divisions, there are sectarian divisions in British Islam based on various groups originating in the Indian sub-continent.

The Barelvis

This is the main sect among British Muslims. It originated with an Indian Sunni Muslim, Raza Khan. He led a reaction against the import of Saudi-Arabian Wahhabism into Indian Islam. The Wahhabis felt that what was wrong with Islam was that it had lost its roots and started to make Muhammad into a semi-divine figure, to worship the graves of saints and follow special holy men. They also rejected the Sufis.

As a reaction against this the Barelvis insist on the role of Muhammad as a semi-divine figure. They claim that he had unique knowledge of the unknown and that he had the light of Muhammad which was derived from God's own light and which existed from the beginning of creation. They have a major celebration on the Prophet's birthday (*Eid Milad un'Nabi*) and their imams are often connected with Pirs (Sufi spiritual guides) who are thought to have special powers.

The main aim of the Barelvi movement is love of the Prophet Muhammad and defence of his honour if it is under attack.

The Deobandis

This group is based on the ideas of the Wahhabis and denies the divine light and unique knowledge of the unknown of Muhammad. They are much less political than the Barelvis and emphasise Islam as a personal rather than a social religion.

The Deobandis have their own mosques which they regard as essential to pass on their view of Islam.

The Tablighi Jamaat

This is an off-shoot of the Deobandis which became disillusioned with the Deobandis' introspection. They want to encourage Muslims to project Islam to the rest of the community. Their founder, Maulana Muhammad Ilyas, gave them a six point programme:

1   profess the faith;

2   perform Salah properly;

3   practise knowledge and remembrance of God;

4   respect all Muslims;

5   have sincere intentions;

6   give time to Islam.

Tablighis can be recognised by the wearing of a cap, beard and a long shirt that is worn over trousers shortened to above the ankles.

The Jamaat-I-Islami

This is essentially a Pakistani political party founded by Mawdudi (1903 - 1979). But as he was concerned with how to make Pakistan a Muslim state, it has great religious overtones. It tends to be most powerful among middle-class Muslims and supporters of Saudi-Arabia.

The basic aim of the Jamaat is to relate acceptance of the Shari'a with a modern democratic type of state. It insists that the law and Islam cannot be separated. However, it has no concept of how Muslims should behave in a non-Muslim democracy and seems to be losing support among the young Muslims.

Nevertheless, because it is essentially a middle-class political party it is the most efficient Muslim organisation in the UK.

Associated with the Jamaat are:- the Muslim Education Trust which is the most effective producer of text books and teaching aids for Muslim schools and the UK Islamic Mission which is a source of suppport for missionary activity.

The Jamaat has close connections with Saudi Arabia who provide the funds for its publishing work.

Shi'as

There are many Shi'as in Britain and they sometimes have their own mosques, but often attend other mosques without letting the members know that they are Shi'a.

Modernisers

A variety of groups are concerned with the problem (initiallly raised in the nineteenth century by the Indian Muslim Muhammad Iqbal) of relating Islam to Western knowledge.

The common theme of these groups is a rejection of the traditional approach to Islam. They tend to emphasise that everything a Muslim should need can be found in the Qur'an alone rather than in Hadith and Law Schools. They are also concerned with relating Islam to such issues as women's rights and the environment.

It is usually in this group that British Muslims (in the sense of Britons who have converted to Islam) are found.

Groups connected with this approach are Ahl-e-Hadith, the Pervaizi, and the Islamic Party of Britain.

The Ahmadiyya

Pakistan has declared this group as non-Muslim, and most British Muslims would agree.

However, they class themselves as Muslims and are often invited into schools to talk about Islam because they speak good English and are very articulate about their beliefs.

They originated in Pakistan as a result of the work of Mirza Ahmad (1836 - 1908) who proclaimed himself the Mahdi and claimed he was called by God to bring a new message which would lead to a new age where all mankind would be given a better standard of living and world peace would emerge.

The Ahmaddiyya teach the equality of women, the need for Muslims to have Western education and the use of Western media techniques in spreading the faith.They have their own mosques.

The Impact of Foreign Sponsorship

Many of the mosques and Muslim organisations in the UK are actually funded from abroad - the Central Mosque and Islamic Cultural Centre in Regents Park is organised by the embassies of Muslim countries in London.

This means that the divisions between Muslim countries (Iran-Iraq, Iraq - Saudi Arabia, Iran - Saudi Arabia etc.) are imposed on the British situation. This can cause conflict within the British Muslim community. According to Iqbal Wahhab in *The Independent* of 16 September 1990, leaders of British Mosques funded by Saudi Arabia were called to a three day conference during the Gulf Conflict in order to be told that they must stop criticising the presence of American troops on the holy soil of Saudi Arabia.

Conclusion

In trying to cope with the pressures of surviving in a non-Muslim society, Muslims have often reacted by going back to what they are familiar with and this has led them to argue with each other rather than seek a common course of action to protect Muslims in the UK.

> The principle of unity is not only essential but crucial to the survival of the Muslim community in Britain. In an anti-Islamic society, a divided Muslim community plays into the hands of those who seek to keep it weak. Disunity is suicidal to the survival of Muslims in Western societies, for a divided community is weak and vulnerable to attacks. (Mohammad Raza)

Problems Faced by the Muslim Community in Britain

1. Education

A major problem for Muslims living in Britain is that their childen have to be educated in the British school system by law until the age of 16. They fear that this will encourage them to become 'westernised'. Muslim parents value education as a way to help their children (especially sons) get on in life. However, most are very worried about the mixing of the sexes, the fact that religion is likely to be denigrated in favour of science and that their children will adopt the life style and attitudes of Western culture. In other words education will cause the children to desert Islam.

They also worry about the social effects. Muslim girls and boys are likely to make friends with non-Muslims and may even want to marry them which is likely to have a disastrous effect on their Muslim faith.

British schools are not likely to give any education in Islam and so their children are likely to grow up knowing more about Christianity than Islam.

2. The Role of Women

Those Muslims who came to Britain from the Indian sub-continent were used to women being in *purdah* (totally separated from men). This is a very different thing in a Muslim society of extended families than it is in a non-Muslim society of predominantly nuclear families.

In Pakistan women have their own social life totally separate from men, but coming to Britain for many Muslim women has meant being trapped in the home on their own. Something many have not been prepared to accept.

Most Muslim families regard daughters as a source of family honour (*izzat*). Boys who date English girls, drink or go to discos may be unIslamic, but they do not affect the family's izzat, whereas a girl who did these things would do so. Consequently, many British Muslims are involved in keeping their daughters away from any form of Western lifestyle. However, education and television mean that girls do become aware of this lifestyle, especially its emphasis on female equality and career hopes for girls.

Muslims are affected by the way of life around them and as they need more money, they realise the need for working wives, but how can their wives work in a mixed workforce where they might not be allowed to wear Muslim dress and would have to work with men?

3. The World of Work

The main pressures on Muslims to be found in the world of work concern Salah and Ramadan. Few employers are likely to provide facilities for performing Salah and it may well be impossible to take a break at the prayertime anyway. This problem can be solved by the practice of combining prayer times when Muslims return home from work. Of much more importance to the Muslim community is Friday Juma prayer. This is the time when the Muslim community should come together and receive the advice and fellowship to enable them to keep true to their faith. However, employers are not likely to give time off for this, especially as the time for Juma prayers varies with the time of sunset so that employers cannot be sure what time their employee will need.

Ramadan imposes special burdens on Muslims in Britain especially those who live in the North and Scotland when Ramadan falls in the summer. Muslims working in heavy industry may well need help because of the fasting prohibition of drinking.

4. Sex and Marriage

The traditional separation of the sexes followed by arranged marriages which is the norm in the Indian sub-continent is causing major problems. As we saw earlier it is almost impossible under the education system to keep the sexes apart. Also the impact of television, education and the media is making young Muslims question the system and seek some way of bringing lovematches into Islam.

5. Social and Economic Life

The Muslim food laws can cause severe problems for Muslims not living within a large Muslim community. Halal butchers are often in short supply and children frequently have difficulties with school meals services being unsympathetic to their needs.

An even greater problem is that of economics. How can a Muslim obey the Qur'anic teaching on interest when living in a society where every bank and building society, every insurance company operates on the interest system ?

Drinking alcohol and gambling can cause a problem for some Muslim men, but there is no reason for this, as it is quite possible to live in a non-Muslim society and not participate in these activities.

6. The Particular Problems of Young Muslims

Most young Muslims have four formative influences on their lives which are often pulling in opposite directions:

Home and parents

Parents who were not brought up in the UK are often poorly educated and trying to impose the customs of an agricultural society on their children. The Muslim community identifies several types of Muslim parents - those strong in belief and practice; those strong in belief and weak in practice; those weak in belief and strong in practice; those weak in belief and practice and indifferent to Islam. Obviously, such parents will produce children with very different attitudes and commitment to Islam.

Mosques, Madrassahs and Islamic Centres

Most parents send their children to these to learn Islam, but they are likely to be: poorly funded; principally for the needs of adult Muslims; run by imams (*mulvis*) who were educated in Pakistan, have little or no knowledge of English and Western culture and teach by rote learning with no concept of understanding.

School

Here they receive minimal information on Islam and what is given will be directed to non-Muslims. The teaching is geared to liberal, rational Christianity and Islam is often shown in a poor light e.g. in history lessons on the Eastern Question. The schools are often insensitive to the needs of Muslim children in terms of dress, PE, food etc.

Society

Throughout their lives Muslim children come into contact with Western material values and lifestyles. This comes primarily from television and friends, but also from newspapers, magazines etc. From this, young Muslims often find it difficult to know their identity and to sort out their own lifestyle.

Parents are very worried that the influence of school and society will lead to their children deserting Islam.

How Islam in Britain is Trying to Deal With the Problems

1: Muslim Organisations

As mentioned earlier there are many Muslim organisations in the UK, most of whom have been established to deal with one or other of the problems facing Muslims in Britain. However, most of these organisations are based on one of the groups in British Islam and/or foreign funded.

The groups which seem most likely to deal with the fundamental problem of making Islam relevant to young people born and brought up in the UK are those which concentrate on Britain rather than harking back to ethnic origins. In particular Dr Zaki Badawi's Muslim College in London which trains imams in Islam from a Western viewpoint and the Murabitun Group which relates Islam to environmental, feminist and racist issues are likely to have significant longterm effects.

Some young Muslims are joining together to produce Muslim magazines to compete with Western magazines (e.g. *Insight* produced in Glasgow and *MuslimWise* produced in London). These present Islam in an attractive and understandable way for young Muslims.

Mohammad Raza feels that the need is for an organisation of mosques which will really represent all Muslims in the UK.

> The mosques - with few exceptions - seem to have compromised Islam in Britain. This important institution is being used for personal interests, and the mosque has not been turned into a community centre which is not only alive to the needs of the Muslim community, but is also directive ... The day that the

mosques start taking an active stance in the affairs of the Muslim community, then the community will be made strong. (Mohammad Raza)

2: Mosques and Madrassahs

One way in which Muslims have reacted to the problems has been to build their own mosques (though many have actually been foreign funded). There are now over one thousand mosques in Britain.

However, many Muslims (see especially Mohammad Raza) feel that there is a need for a drastic overhaul of mosque functions, which is now happening in some mosques.

Rather than being just a place for Salah and the madrassah for teaching the Qur'an, they should become a Muslim centre. Youth club facilities should be provided for both girls and boys; a structured teaching of Islam and Arabic should be provided for children using proven educational methods; facilities should be provided for women to meet and learn English; apart from Arabic, English should be the language of the mosque.

At the moment many mosques are simply places for older male Muslims, the type of reforms Raza suggests would change this character and give Muslims a centre of identity and action. It would also allow the extension of what is already happening in some mosques where savings co-operatives allow Muslims to buy houses and bank without being involved in interest.

Perhaps most importantly of all for Muslim communities, it would give a springboard for political participation. The way this can be done has been outlined in Dr Neilsen's, *A Survey of Local Authority Responses to Muslim Needs*. This sums up what Muslims are doing around the country and could be a blueprint for how local mosques could become politically aware:

1   Burial - negotiate Muslim areas in cemeteries and Muslim methods of burial.

2   Slaughter - negotiate facilities for halal slaughter of cattle and poultry.

3   Education - discuss provision of school facilities for Muslim Instruction; single sex schools; school meals and Muslim dietary laws; school uniform; policies on PE and sex education.

4   Worship - negotiate time off for festivals and Juma prayers for Muslims employed by the local authority.

5   Literacy - negotiate a literacy programme for Asian women and the provision of library books for Asian language users.

This would provide a sense of Muslim identity and make the local mosques have democratic elections of representatives. It is already happening in many areas.

3: Publications

Most of the Muslim publishers are not producing books of a similar printing and layout standard to other British publications. Muslim newspapers, magazines and books should use Western techniques so that the message is not ignored because the packaging is inferior.

Conclusion

Islam in the UK is organised on ethnic and sectarian lines which reflect the national origins and concerns of immigrants rather than second and third generation Muslims. This makes it difficult to cope with the challenges facing the younger generation of Muslims.

There are many indications, however, that this situation is changing and if the new generation of British Muslims start to adopt the approaches outlined above, the situation could become much easier for young British Muslims.

In the British culture the Islamic alternative has to be presented in an attractive manner which will not only raise the self-image of Muslims but also offer salvation to Westerners. This has not received any attention because the Muslim community is still engrossed in its petty disputes and does not even project a clear-cut worldview and perspective of Islam. The present face of Islam is sufficient to drive away non-Muslims from Islam. In order to present Islam as a powerful alternative to the dominant tradition and powerful Western civilisation, it has to be presented in an equally attractive manner. It has to be a self-sufficient package of a civilisation within a civilisation which comprises much more than the five pillars of Islam, (Mohammad Raza).

GLOSSARY OF ARABIC WORDS

Eid al'Adha (Id ul'Adha)   the festival of sacrifice in Dhu al'Hijja

Adhan (Azan)   the call to prayer

Akirah   belief in the Final Judgement and life after death

Allah   Arabic for God

Amin   trustworthy

Ansar   the first Medinan Muslims

Aqiqa   the naming ceremony for Muslim babies

Al'Ashura   the Shi'a festival remembering the martyrdom of Husayn

Ayat   a verse of the Qur'an

Ayatollah   literally sign of God, the name given to Shi'a religious leaders (chief mujtahids) in Iran

Bab   literally 'gate 'used by Shi'as for one in contact with the Hidden Imam

Barzakh   period between death and the Final Judgement

Berakah   grace

Biraderi   Pakistani, Bangladeshi and Indian Muslim form of caste

Bismillah   the introduction to every sura except 9 ('In the name of God the Merciful, the Compassionate')

Dajjal   the beast who will come at the end of the world

Darud   prayers of blessing on the prophets

Dhu al'Hijja   the twelfth month of the Islamic calendar when Hajj takes place

Din	religion, especially Islam
Du'a	personal as opposed to ritual prayers
Eid (Id)	festival
Faj'r	early morning prayers
Fana	the Sufi passing away into God trance
Fard	compulsory
Fatiha	the first sura of the Qur'an
Fatwa	a legal decision for Muslims to follow
Fiqh	the science of Muslim law
Eid al'Fit'r (Id ul'Fit'r)	the festival of the end of Ramadan celebrated on the 1 Shawwal
Ghadir al'Khum	the Shi'a festival celebrating Muhammad appointing Ali as his successor
Ghusl	the ritual washing of the whole body
Hadith (Ahadith)	a saying of Muhammad
Hadith Qudsi	a hadith which was directly inspired by God
Hafiz	a Muslim who has memorised the whole Qur'an
Hajj	pilgrimage to Mecca in Dhu al'Hijja
Hajji	someone who has successfully completed the Hajj
Hal	Sufi mystical state
Halal (Hallal)	lawful, permitted for Muslims
Hanif	Arab monotheist before Muhammad
Haram	that which is forbidden to Muslims
Hijab	Muslim dress particularly for women
Hijra	the emigration of Muhammad to Medina from Mecca
Houri	a heavenly companion of the righteous
Ibadah	worship

Ihram	pilgrim dress
Ijtahid	interpretation of the Shari'a to solve new problems
Ilm	special knowledge of the Shi'a Imams
Imam (Urdu - *Mulvi*)	Sunni prayer leader, Shi'a successor of the Prophet with special powers
Iman	faith
Injil	the Gospel revealed to Isa
Insh'Allah	if God wills
Iqama	personal call to prayer
Isha	late evening prayer
Isnad	line of guarantors for the validity of a Hadith
Izzat	family honour
Jahanna	hell
Jahiliyya	days of ignorance
Jama'at	prayers said in congregation in the mosque
Janazah	Salah prayers for funerals
al'Jannah	heaven
Jihad (Jehad)	struggle in the way of God
Jinn	spirits of the desert who can be good or evil
Juma	Friday midday congregational prayers
Ka'ba (Ka'aba)	the House of God in Mecca
Khalifa (Caliph)	successor of Muhammad
Khamr	intoxicants forbidden by the Qur'an
Khutba	sermon
Kiswan	the black covering of the Ka'ba
Kitab	book (used in the Qur'an to refer to the Qur'an)
Kuf'r (Kaffir)	unbelief

Madrassah	Muslim school (usually next to the mosque)
Maghrib	prayer after sunset
Mahr	money given by groom to bride as part of the marriage contract
Mahdi	the one that defeats Dajjal at the end of the world. Sunnis say it will be Isa, while Shi'a say it will be the Hidden Imam
Makruh	actions disapproved of by Islam but not punishable
Mandub	actions recommended by Islam but not compulsory
Maqam	Sufi prayer techniques
Maruf	right, good
Ma'sa	covered walkway between the hills Safa and Marwa in Mecca
Masjid	see Mosque
Mawali	non-Arab Muslims
Mihrab	niche in the wall of the mosque indicating the direction of Mecca
Eid Milad al'Nabi	festival of the Prophet's birthday
Mosque (Masjid)	place of prostration
Mubah	actions about which the Shari'a is silent
Muezzin	person who calls the faithful to prayer
Mufti	Muslim lawyer
Muhajirun	the Meccan Companions of the Prophet who emigrated to Medina with him
Mujheedin (Mujahidin)	one struggling for God
Mujaddid	renewer of the faith who Shi'as believe will be sent at the beginning of every century
Mujtahid	Shi'a religious lawyer and leader
Munafiqun	hypocrites who only pretend to be Muslims
Munkar	evil

Muslim	one who has submitted to the will of God
Muta	the Shi'a practice of temporary marriage
Mu'tazilite	eighth-century theologians who believed in free will and rejected al'Qadr and the physical characteristics of God
Nabi	prophet
Nafrillah	optional raka't during Salah
Nass	the Shi'a belief that each Imam appointed his successor
Nisab	the amount you can earn before being liable to Zakah
Niyya	prayer of intent before Salah
Purdah	the separation of women
Qadi	judge
al'Qadr	belief in God's control of events
Qibla	direction of prayer
Qurra	the first soldiers of Islam
Raka (pl. Raka't)	the set of actions that make up Salah prayer
Ramadan	the ninth Muslim month when all Muslims must fast
Rasul	messenger of God
Riba	lending money at interest
Ridda	the Arab tribes who deserted Islam after Muhammad's death
Risalah	belief in prophets (including angels and holy books
Ruku	bowing in the direction of the Ka'ba during Salah
Sadaqah	voluntary charity giving
Sadiq	truthful
Salaam	peace
Salah (Salat) (Urdu - *Namaas*)	ritual prayer

Sawm	fasting
Sa'y	running seven times along the Ma'sa during Hajj and umra
Shahada(h) (Urdu - *Kalima*)	confession of Muslim faith
Shari'a	the Muslim law of God
Sharif	a chief mufti
Shawwal	tenth Muslim month
Shaykh (Urdu - *Pir*)	Shi'a religious leader
Shi'a (Shi'i, Shi'ite)	party of Ali, those Muslims who believe in successors of Muhammad starting from Ali
Shirk	associating other beings or things with God
Shura	the early electoral college for choosing the Khalifa
Sifat	God's omniscience
Sufi	Muslim mystic
Suhur	meal before dawn during Ramadan
Sujud	prostration during Salah
Sunna	example or way of life of Muhammad
Sunni	Muslim who follows the Sunna of Muhammad
Sura	a chapter of the Qur'an
Takbir	the repetition of God is great
Talaq	divorce when only the man wants it
Talbiya	special prayer on Hajj
Taqiyya	the Shi'a practice of pretendiong to be another religion if you are threatened by religious persecution
Tarawih	extra Salah night prayers during Ramadan
Tariqa	a Sufi way
Tashahhud	prayer for peace on those around you during Salah

Tawaf	walking round the Ka'ba during Hajj or umra
Tawhid	belief in God's unity
Tawrat	the Torah revealed to Musa
Ulama	group of Muslim lawyers
Umma	the Muslim community
Umra	the lesser pilgrimage where you go to Mecca outside the month of Hajj and do tawak and sa'y in ihram
Wahhabis	puritanical Muslim sect of Saudi Arabia
Wali	guardian
Waquf	standing prayer during Hajj
Witr	three sunna rakat during Isha prayers
Wudu (Wuzu)	ritual washing during Salah
Zabur	the book of Psalms revealed to Dawud
Zakah (Zakat)	compulsory charity giving
Zina	sex outside marriage
Zuhr	midday prayers

RECOMMENDED READING

GENERAL RECOMMENDED READING

Glasse, Cyril, *The Concise Encyclopaedia of Islam*, Stacey International, 1989.

Mawdudi, Abul Ala, *Towards Understanding Islam*, Islamic Foundation, 1980.

Sarwar, Ghulam, *Islam: Beliefs and Teachings*, Muslim Education Trust, 1989.

CHAPTER 1 - THE QUR'AN

Gatje, Helmut, *The Qur'an and its Exegesis*, Routledge, 1976.

Ibrahim and Davies, (trans), *An'Nawari's Forty Hadith*, Holy Koran Publishing House, 1976.

Irving, Ahmad and Ahsan, *The Qur'an - Basic Teachings*, Islamic Foundation, 1990.

Mustafa, Muhammad, *Studies in Hadith Methodology and Literature*, American Trust Publications, 1977.

Nasr, Seyyed Hossein, (ed.), *Islamic Spirituality* Routledge, 1987, the following chapters; 'The Qur'an as the Foundation of Islamic Spirituality', Seyyed Hossein Nasr; 'The Spiritual Significance of the Qur'an' Allahbakhsh K. Brohi.

Rippin, Andrew, *Muslims their Religious Beliefs and Practices Volume 1*, Routledge, 1990.

CHAPTER 2 - THE SIX BELIEFS OF ISLAM

Bucaille, Maurice, *The Qur'an and Modern Science*, Islamic Propogation Centre, 1989.

Nasr, Seyyed Hossein, (ed.), *Islamic Spirituality*, Routledge, 1987, the following chapters; 'God', Seyyed Hossein Nasr; 'The Angels', Sachiko Murata; 'Eschatology', William C. Chittick; 'The Cosmos and the

Natural Order', Seyyed Hossein Nasr.

Thomson, Ahmad, *Dajjal The King who has no clothes*, TA-HA, 1986.

CHAPTER 3 - THE FIVE PILLARS OF ISLAM

Ahmad, Kurshid, (ed.), *Islam its Meaning and Message*, Islamic Foundation, 1980, the following chapters; 'The Islamic Concept of Worship', Mustafa Ahmad al'Zarqa; 'Islam Basic Principles and Characteristics', Kurshid Ahmad.

Kamal, Ahmad, *The Sacred Journey*, Allen and Unwin, 1964.

Khan, Zafa-ul-Islam and Zaki, Yaqub (eds), *Hajj in Focus*, Open Press, 1986.

Nasr, Seyyed Hossein, (ed.), *Islamic Spirituality*, Routledge, 1987, the following chapters; 'The Inner Meaning of the Islamic Rites', Syed Ali Ashraf; 'The Spiritual Dimension of Prayer', Allahbakhsh K. Brohi.

von Grunebaum, G.E., *Muhammadan Festivals*, Curzon Press, 1976, (some good quotes from Muslims despite the appalling title!).

CHAPTER 4 - THE SHARI'A AND THE MUSLIM WAY OF LIFE

al'Qaradawi, Yusuf, *The Lawful and the Prohibited in Islam*, American Trust Publications, 1960.

Donohue and Esposito, (eds), *Islam in Transition*, Oxford University Press, 1982, the following chapters; 'Adaptation of Islamic Jurisprudence to Modern Social Needs', Subhi Mahmasani; 'The Re-interpretation of Islam', Asaf Fyzee; 'Fatwa on Family Planning in Islam', Shaykh Abdullah al'Qalqili; 'Islamic Economics: Ownership and Tawhid', Abul Hasan Bani-Sadr.

Lemu, Aisha and Hearen, Fatima, *Women in Islam*, Islamic Foundation, 1978.

Pearl, David, *A Textbook of Muslim Personal Law*, Croom Helm, 1987.

CHAPTER 5 - THE LIFE OF THE PROPHET

Ahmad, Kurshid, (ed.), *Islam its Meaning and Message*, Islamic Foundation, 1980, the chapter,'The Life of the Prophet Muhammad', Abd'al Rahman Azzam.

Cook, Michael, *Muhammad*, Oxford, 1983.

Lewis, Bernard, *The Arabs in History*, Hutchinson, 1970, (chapters 1 and 2).

Nasr, Seyyed Hossein, *Islamic Spirituality*, Routledge, 1987, the chapter,'The Life of the Prophet', Ja'far Qasimi.

Rao, K.S. Ramakrishna, *Muhammad The Prophet of Islam*, Islamic Propagation Centre, 1985.

Rippin, Andrew, *Muslims their Religious Beliefs and Practices, Volume 1*, Routledge, 1990.

Rodinson, Maxime, *Mohammed*, Penguin, 1971.

Shaban, M.A., *Islamic History - a New Interpretation*, Cambridge University Press, 1971, (Chapter 1).

Watt, Montgomery, *Muhammad, Prophet and Statesman*, Oxford, 1960.

CHAPTER 6 - A BRIEF HISTORY OF ISLAM

Aziz, M.A., *A History of Pakistan*, Sang-e-Meel Publications, Lahore, 1979.

Cantwell Smith, Wilfred, *Islam in Modern History*, Mentor Books, 1957.

Donohue and Esposito, (eds), *Islam in Transition*, Oxford University Press, 1982, the following chapters; 'The Caliphate and the Bases of Power', Ali Abd al'Raziq; 'Muslim Unity and Arab Unity', Sati al'Husri.

Lewis, Bernard, *The Arabs in History*, Hutchinson, 1970.

Rippin, Andrew, *Muslims their Religious Beliefs and Practices, Volume 1*, Routledge, 1990.

Savory, R.M.,(ed.), *An Introduction to Islamic Civilisation*, Cambridge University Press, 1976, the chapter, 'The Historical Background of Islamic Civilisation', C.E. Bosworth.

Shaban, M.A., *Islamic History - a New Interpretation*, Cambridge, 1971.

Sutherland, Houlden, Clarke and Hardy,(eds),*The World's Religions* , Routledge, 1988, the following chapters; 'Early Islam', Julian Baldick; 'Islam in the Indian Sub-Continent', F.A. Nizami; 'Islam in Contemporary Europe', Peter Clarke; 'Islam in North America', S.S. Nyang.

The Cambridge History of Islam, Volumes 1 and 2, Cambridge University Press, 1970.

CHAPTER 7 - DIFFERENCES IN ISLAM

Haeri, Shaykh Fadhalla, *The Elements of Sufism*, Element Books, 1990.

Lings, Martin, *What is Sufism?*, Allen and Unwin, 1975.

Momen, Moojan, *An Introduction to Shi'i Islam*, Yale University Press, 1985.

Nicholson, R.A., *The Mystics of Islam*, Routledge, 1963.

Shah, Idries, *The Way of the Sufi*, Penguin, 1968.

CHAPTER 8 - ISLAM IN BRITAIN

Badham, P.,(ed.), *Religion State and Society in Modern Britain*, Edwin Mellen Press, 1989, the chapter 'Islamic Communities in Britain', Jorgen S. Nielsen.

Gerholm and Lithman,(eds), *The New Islamic Presence in Western Europe*, Mansell, 1988.

Raza, Mohammad S., *Islam in Britain - Past, Present and the Future*, Volcano Press, 1991.

INDEX